Won
Emel

D1333936

£7.99

The author, Herbert Andrew, a young police lieutenant then.
He joined the Malayan Police Force in 1950 on a three year contract.

WHO WON THE MALAYAN EMERGENCY?

HERBERT ANDREW

Graham Brash
Singapore

First published in 1995 by
Graham Brash (Pte) Ltd
32 Gul Drive
Singapore 2262

ISBN 981-218-047-8

The author and the publishers would like to thank the Gurkha
Museum in Winchester, U.K., for use of the photographs on pp. 40
& 41. All other photographs in the book are courtesy of the author.

Cover photo courtesy of Herbert Andrew
Cover designed by Gael Lee
Typeset by Syarikat Broadway Typesetting Sdn. Bhd.
Printed in Singapore by Vine Graphic Pte Ltd

Contents

Preface

This is an account of the Malayan Emergency during the years 1950 –1955 as seen through the eyes of a former police lieutenant who was with the Malayan police at that time.

He describes the bloody battles between the terrorists and the security forces and gives his own opinion of the background to the Emergency and the part played by the police, the Chinese, the Malays, the Gurkhas, General Templer and the security forces.

Many of the accounts are described in a light-hearted way but the underlying horrors of the Emergency run through the book from the beginning to the end.

(Editor's Note: The publishers will not be held responsible for the views expressed in this book as they are the author's personal views.)

1. Introduction

Malaya is a small country about the same size as England and is geographically situated just north of the equator. The island of Singapore which at that time was part of Malaya is now an independent country, positioned on the equator and connected to the mainland of Malaya by a bridge known locally as the Causeway.

In recent times the countries and states of Sarawak, North Borneo and Brunei have gone into partnership with the old mainland Malaya and formed the new country now known as Malaysia. Singapore is, as we have said, an independent country, but still remains part of the British Commonwealth of Nations.

The Malays and the Sakai are the original peoples of Malaya, with the Malays living in the cities, towns and kampongs and the Sakai living in the jungle and on the jungle fringes. The population of Malaya was about five million at that time and over 50% was Malay and the remainder Chinese, Indian and European. There were only about 10,000 Europeans but the number increased when the troops arrived to help in the fight against the terrorists.

The Chinese, the Indians and the British immigrated into Malaya between 1800 and 1950 and because the British were a strong military power, they made Malaya part of the British Empire.

Despite the number of different races and religions in Malaya, harmony and prosperity developed during those early years. Singapore became the centre of world trade in the area and Malaya, being a leading rubber and tin producer, was a leading light in the commerce of Southeast Asia. Chinese, Malay, Indian, European, who were Christians, Buddhists,

Muslims and many other religions and races got on very well together and, above all, they all loved their beautiful Malaya.

Unfortunately, it was too good to last and when the ruthless Japanese army arrived in 1942 they turned this pleasant land into an evil concentration camp. All of the people of Malaya were terrorised, tortured and many thousands were killed by these cruel, heartless, ruthless invaders.

A few hundred, probably no more than one thousand of the local people, British, Chinese, Indians, and Pakistanis started to organise themselves into groups in the jungle and their efforts were backed by the "start up" dumps of arms and food which some thoughtful people had set up inside the jungle against the possible happening of an invasion by the Japanese.

The British called themselves Force 136 and when joined together with the others, they were jointly called the MPAJA (the Malayan People's Anti-Japanese Army). In the early days of the war the Communist Party had begun to get organised in both the mainland and Singapore and by the time the Japanese had arrived, they too had organised themselves both inside and outside the jungle against such an eventuality.

As the occupation continued the two groups of Communists and MPAJA merged into one organisation. The Communists earned their living by threatening the local people and when in camp had daily lectures on the principles of Communism. The Communists were the leaders of the gangs and these political leaders always made the final decisions. The rank and file members took no part in the decision making and just had to obey all orders. The British element was responsible for all the training and the care of arms and ammunition. During the war from 1941 to 1945 these groups fought a running battle against the Japanese, had some success and suffered a lot of hardship. The book *The Jungle is Neutral* by Col. Spencer Chapman (which I must confess to having read three times), gives an accurate account of the battles which the MPAJA had with the Japanese in these years.

Chin Peng was the Secretary General of the Communists during the Emergency, which started in 1948, he was 26 years old and born in Sitiawan in Malaya. He was well educated and spoke five or six languages, including English. As Ho Chih Minh was to the Vietnamese Communists, so was Chin Peng to the Malayan Communists. Have no doubt about one thing and that is that Chin Peng was his own man and took no instructions from China or Moscow. He received his instructions in jungle warfare from the British instructors of Force 136 as did many of the Communists. Chin Peng numbered many British amongst his friends. When the war against the Japanese had been won, Chin Peng took part in the victory parade in London as an honoured guest of the British government but when he returned to Malaya he still had political ambitions to rule Malaya as a Communist leader and to have a Communist government. He got very little support for his ambition and for his ideology and so Chin Peng went back to the jungle and started a war against his friends, the British. One day he was fighting with the British and the next, he was fighting against them. The Emergency started because Chin Peng thought that it would be a fairly easy matter to beat the British for had he not played a major role in defeating the Japanese? He reasoned that the British and the Malays should not be too difficult to beat. With the assistance of the Min Yuen (Chinese helpers in most villages and towns) he thought that the battle could be won and he could make Malaya into a Communist country.

The Communist army of Malaya was organised along military lines and divided into regiments, companies and platoons and they commenced operations in 1948 by systematically killing the British rubber estate managers. In the first year of the Emergency, several hundred were killed. They followed up these successes by killing policemen and local civilians by the hundreds and in less than one year they had terrorised the nation.

They were called CTs, which is short for Communist Terrorists. They were mostly Chinese, some educated, others uneducated. Some of them were just local Chinese ruffians who were making a living stealing from the local people and if they had to kill a few whilst they were stealing that was just unfortunate for the ones who died. In short, some of the terrorists were just local gangsters who just didn't care much about what they did or who suffered whilst they were doing it. It was thought that the official leadership of the terrorists were in contact with Communist China and received their instructions from them, but as far as I am aware, this was just a theory. Many of them were the remains of the MPAJA and the others, the majority, were local Chinese men and women who were forced to join under threat of death if they refused. Their arms and equipment were not good and they had to steal arms and ammunition from the local security forces whenever they could. They were supported by their local Min Yuen followers (local networks of food suppliers and information givers) some of whom were dressed in half military style uniforms but were usually armed with just pistols and a few grenades. The discipline was strict and there were many rules that had to be obeyed. Those who did not obey the terrorist leaders' rules usually died in front of a firing squad. Their leaders at every level of command were politically motivated Communists. They wanted power and, in trying to obtain that power, they used the services of many local Chinese whether they wanted to help or not.

They were ruthless and killed and tortured many thousands of local people during the Emergency and whether you were Malay, Chinese, Indian or European you would die if you stood in their way. During the Emergency days the whole country almost slept with one eye open, for the terrorists had informants everywhere and you could be next on their hit list. Their jungle patrols or platoons were made up of about 30 or 40 Chinese men and youths and some women and girls who, from experience, we found were more fanatical than the men if they were in a tight corner. Their uniform was khaki shirt and trousers like the Army wore in China and khaki hat with peaks and a red cloth star on the front which again was similar to the uniform of mainland China regular troops. Also like the Chinese army they wore khaki puttees wound around their legs from knee to ankle.

Who would fight them?

The Malays would fight them.

It was their country, wasn't it? Who lived in all the kampongs (villages), the Malays lived there and their leaders were Malay. Their sultans were Malay, so it was their country and they would fight for it. If the terrorists were to win, then it would have to be done over the dead bodies of the Malay people, that is how they felt and that is how they behaved. Malays are quiet and very slow to show anger, but they were reliable and steadfast and over a period of time they used their patience and reliability against the ruthless enemy.

When the Emergency was eventually over, there were many Malays numbered amongst the honoured dead. They had fought bravely for Malaya and for this they will always be remembered by those who survived those dangerous days.

The Malayan Communist Party was similar to most communist parties in other parts of the world. They were utterly ruthless and their message of "equal shares for all" led many people up the garden path, but in reality, once they had achieved power as they did in Russia and China they imprisoned their populations under a set of rigid rules and their leaders lived in comfort. Once suppressed by the yoke of Communism few emerged again as free spirits. The MCP had started to organise themselves to compete for political power long before the Japanese arrived. Their method, well tested by other Communists throughout the world, was to ferment industrial and social unrest amongst the population wherever and whenever they got the chance.

These well tested methods make an interesting subject, but perhaps the most simple way to explain their system is to say that they systematically ferment greed into the hearts of the working people so that they become jealous of the possessions which other people had obtained and the successes which they had achieved in their lives. When the Japanese arrived in 1942 the Malayan Communist parties hid in the jungles of Malaya and in obscurity in Singapore and other Communist parties in nearby countries did the same. In Malaya, they existed in jungle camps and were supported and fed by the Chinese population of the area.

The British Force 136 provided their military training (even though their numbers were small) and jointly they "hung on" together until the British came back in 1945. Force 136 and the MCP made strange "bed fellows" during the Japanese occupation. Force 136 struggled to keep alive depite continuous attacks of malaria and other sicknesses and when their health was good they trained the Communist recruits. The Communists just talked and talked and talked, mostly about the glory of Communism and the evils of Western Democracy. They were of course not the whole of the MPAJA effort. There were many independent companies, and platoons who operated independently of Communist influence and as we have said they did a lot better against the Japanese than the others who were commanded by politicians. These "independent" units were ridiculed by the Communist Terrorists who referred to them as "bandits" or "guerrillas" which they used in an insulting and derogatory way. The independent units also never lost a chance to ridicule the CTs whenever they could.

The 16th of June 1948 marked the start of the Emergency which was to last for twelve years. Communism has been spreading in Southeast Asia since 1925 and the main aim of the Malayan Communist Party was to seize power in Malaya from the British. A lot of arms and ammunition had been stored by the MPAJA so that they could eventually be used against the British and of course a lot of time had been spend training the Chinese recruits to hate the British and love Communism. You must make this distinction with the Chinese, whether it was in the war against the Japanese, or in the Emergency against the Malays and the British. In both conflicts there were just a few diehard Communists in their gangs whilst the large majority of the Chinese were there by accident. By this I mean they were either bullied into being members of the CT units or they were just local "no goods" who would join anything, anywhere, anytime.

In recent times Russia was the first country to accept Communism as a way of life and as a method of government. China quickly followed this example and so Communist China was formed. Other countries that were situated near Russia, became satellites to the two great powers.

As Communism developed there were some countries who rejected the Communist way of life and one of these countries was Malaya.

The country of Malaya had only limited numbers of their own security forces and largely depended on Britain if any emergency should arise. Such an emergency did arise in 1948. The enemy were Communist terrorists, who, inspired by the success of Communism in China, had set themselves up in the jungle all over the Malayan mainland. Malaya had a population of five or six million about this time. They were roughly divided into half Chinese and half Malay with a few thousand Indians, Europeans and Pakistanis. Because most of the terrorists were Chinese, the Chinese civilians were reluctant to join the security forces. That only left the Malays and a few thousand Indians and Pakistanis to take up the struggle. The Malays are not naturally aggressive and tend to be friendly, shy and easy going. It suited them to be like this, but if they were to combat Communism they would have to change their way of life and change it quickly. If they didn't, the Communists would quickly take over their country and all their culture would be lost. The Malays seemed to instinctively know this and very soon thousands of them joined the Malayan police as Special Constables.

So there we have it, a few battalions of British and Gurkha troops, two or three battalions of Malay Regiment and the peace-loving Malays.

It is probably true to say that in 1950 the terrorist numbers were probably larger than the security forces numbers. Malaya looked set to fight a losing battle. The Malayan government, through the "Crown Agents" in London, began to recruit British civilians as Police Lieutenants to strengthen the Malayan police.

2. Frank Barron and Charles Thornton

Frank Barron

Frank Barron had been brought up in the backstreets of the east end of London and learnt his lessons about life the hard way. His father was unemployable because he was a drunkard and the family existed on the money which his mother earned doing washing and ironing for other people who lived in the area.

Frank joined a gang of local boys when he was about ten years old and by the time he was sixteen had graduated into one of the biggest "daredevils" in the area. He was not afraid to fight anyone anytime, and at sixteen could generally be described as stockily built. Luckily for Barron, the Army accepted him as a recruit Boy Soldier and though his seniors found him difficult to handle, he had graduated to the Army as a Private by the time he was eighteen years of age.

It was an Infantry battalion and in 1947 he was posted to Palestine (now Israel) to help in the war against the Zionist terrorists who wanted to take over the country for themselves. He was good at the job and first made the rank of Corporal and then was promoted to Acting Sergeant.

He was happy enough with army life but when he found that he could speak Arabic quite well and get along with the local people, he wondered if there was a way of benefiting from his new-found talent.

There was not a lot to do in Jerusalem at night, for the local girls had been warned about bothering soldiers, so it was usually an Arab bar which attracted the trade of the troops after dark.

On this particular night, he had drunk more than his quota of the local beer which had led to a couple of encounters with three other soldiers in the bar. He was slumping heavily in a chair at a table in the bar thinking about what his next move would be if the other soldiers troubled him again when a hand was placed firmly on his right shoulder and an English voice with a London East End accent said "Steady down, mate. I think you've had enough".

The talker was a Palestine police sergeant whose face seemed a little familiar. "Don't you recognise me, Barron?" said the Palestine policeman, "We've had a few together in the Bull down the Old Kent Road; I remember you very well for you helped me out in a punch-up one night."

Barron went with the Palestine police sergeant who saw him safely back to his barracks. After Drill Parade the following day he lay on his bed and tried to reassemble the events of the previous night. Yes, the policeman's face was familiar, but that was about all, he certainly couldn't put a name to the face or recall any of the incidents in The Bull down the East End.

A few evenings later, Frank was walking with two of his army friends through one of the "seedier" areas of town when he spotted two policemen surrounded by at least a dozen local roughnecks and were obviously having a hard time. The policemen saw Barron and his friends and shouted to attract their attention. The odds were high, but as we know, Barron liked a fight and his friends weren't cowards. They ran towards the crowd, punched and kicked two or three of them and the rest of them just turned and ran.

By a strange coincidence, one of the policemen was the one who had rescued him from the bar a few evenings earlier. They became friends and when they could both get off duty at the same time they went out together to soak up the local atmosphere and probably the local beer also.

The war against the terrorists in Palestine was hotting up and when Barron got a chance to join the Palestine police as Sergeant, he took it with both hands. But the war against the terrorists was only a short one. A "political" solution was found which left the Arabs without a homeland and Barron without a job. But as we know, fortune always shines on the brave and within a few weeks he and a few dozen other sergeants were transferred to Malaya and joined the Malayan police as Police Lieutenants.

This was in 1949 and there were to be some more surprises around the corner for our tough East Ender.

The Emergency had only been going on in Malaya for a few months when they arrived and the ex-Palestine policemen were the first to be appointed to that rank. The regular police force consisted of gazetted officers which included such ranks as Superintendents at the top and lower down Inspectors and, finally, the Policemen. The British army was there in smallish numbers and the Malay regiment could put out one or two battalions if they were pressed. It was mostly "it will all be over by Christmas" attitude in those early days and the only people in the firing line were the rubber planters. Though total casualties on both sides were some 500 in 1949, the threat was not taken too seriously in those early days.

The police went wild and recruited a few hundred Special Constables to help defend the planters and to provide troops for the new police lieutenants, otherwise it was business as usual in the police stations and the army barracks. Things got worse and more British troops arrived and two battalions of Gurkhas. The Commissioner of Police was changed twice, two battalions of Malay regiment became five and by the middle of 1950 the situation was desperate. Meanwhile, Chin Peng (the Bandit Supremo) had, as we said, recruited many thousands more helpers and fighters.

The Malayan government decided to recruit 400 more police lieutenants from Britain. They all came in during the last half of 1950 and during 1951. Police Lieutenant Barron was posted to Pahang.

Charles Thornton

"You, new fellow, what's your name?" said one of the boarders who was leaning nonchalantly against the college gates as if he was a permanent fixture. The new boy's courage seemed to leave him, but he hoped that his reply sounded confident. This was Charles Thornton's first day at Marlborough, a good public school on the outskirts of Cambridge, England. "Charles Thornton, Sir" he replied. He thought he'd better say 'sir' for the youth was at least two years older than him and was obviously an old hand.

He went into the school hall and introduced himself to the senior master present who seemed to be expecting him by the casual way he ticked his name off a long list. "The dinner bell will be going soon, when you've had dinner come back and see me again and I'll tell you what room you will be in". Charles hardly remembered going into his dormitory that night and even had no recall of who he was sharing it with. He must have slept and slept very well for, as the morning sunlight streamed across his bed, his body seemed unable to stir from its deeply relaxed state, sleep, oh, how delicious it was.

His first year at Marlborough passed quite quickly (they had allowed him to start in the third) for apart from studies during the day and "fagging" most of the evening for senior boys, nothing much seemed to happen. Fagging was more than just going to the local "outdoor" for bread, cheese, butter and, of course, beer and even cigarettes and cheroots sometimes. You'd better be quick or the fifth and sixth form Seniors would beat you around the ears and then their rooms had to be kept tidy and their shoes cleaned. Thank goodness that when you were a Senior you could dispense orders and justice in exactly the same way. This was Marlborough's way of building character into the young men. The masters imparted the knowledge during normal school hours but the real character building went on at night as you sweated on shoe cleaning or running for more bread for the third time in less than half an hour. It seemed to provide most of its products with an inbuilt confidence that could rarely be ruffled.

Thornton progressed well with his studies and played rugby for Marlborough in his final year. He was eighteen years old now and most of his friends were moving on to University. He felt that he did not want to do this. He was well built and could move quickly when he had to; he was also full of energy and a sense of adventure. No, he couldn't settle down to University, not yet, maybe not ever.

All his life he had felt detached from his father who worked as a diplomat for the government in London and the letters from home always came from his mother and most weeks he would write to her and let her know what was happening to him. She was a pillar of strength for him to lean on in difficult times.

The Crown Agents for the Colonies, 4 Millbank, London, etc. – were advertising for persons from the age of eighteen to serve in the Far East. It would be a dangerous job said the interviewing officer, but it would be for three years and they'd give him a contract. That's how Charles Thornton got himself to Singapore with those other raw police lieutenants and had the temerity to announce to us all that he was worried about not getting a letter from his mummy. We laughed at him but it didn't ruffle his hard Marlborough confidence. He joined the rest of us and was eventually posted to Tranum, in the State of Pahang.

*　　*　　*　　*　　*　　*

Police Lieutenant Frank Barron arrived in the town of Mentakab in August 1949 and was immediately put in charge of the Mentakab jungle squad.

There were plenty of terrorists in the area for it was within ten miles of the Pahang river which was the "happy hunting ground" of the Malay Communist terrorists and to the west and southwest were Karak and Kampong Manchis which harboured large groups of Chinese Communist terrorists.

Frank Barron had a very busy time there and got very good results.

The same could be said for Police Lieutenant Charles Thornton who was, as we have said, posted to Tranum Police Station which was about sixty miles north of Mentakab. Most of the bandits around there were in the Raub area which was only about six miles from Tranum. The police lieutenant in charge of the Tranum Police Station jungle squad, the public school boy, built himself up quite a reputation. He arrived late in 1950 and by now the police lieutenants were arriving thick and fast. By the middle of 1951 most of the 500 or so of them had arrived and were hard at work. The country needed them and they set about their task with grim determination.

3. Pahang

If you want to get to the state of Pahang from Kuala Lumpur you have to go up the Genting Road to Bentong and then go through Karak to Mentakab which is more or less in the centre of Pahang. Most of Malaysia is covered in jungle and rubber plantations but Pahang is positioned right in the centre of the country and has more deep jungle than most other parts of Malaya. There are wild animals in the Pahang jungle that you probably wouldn't find in other parts such as elephants, orang utans and panther, but perhaps the most outstanding feature is the river, the Pahang River. It runs through the centre of the state from north of Kuala Lipis mostly in a southeasterly direction and finally turning east for its last glide to the sea on Malaysia's east coast at the town of Pekan. To the east and west of the river are high mountains rising to 5,000 feet in parts and covered with thick jungle. On either side of the last 100 miles of the river's flow to the sea was "bandit country" (the security forces always called the Communist Terrorists "bandits"). Not Chinese bandits as one would normally find in most other parts of the country, but **Malay** bandits. There were at least two very large gangs of Malay bandits led by Malays and probably the most active were the gangs which operated around the kampongs of Mengkarak, Bera, Chenor, Pesagi, Kinchir and Batu Bulis. They were all on the river-side and near to Temerloh where the Malays came to sell their rubber and other things such as fruit and vegetables that they grew near to their kampongs. They lived relatively safely in their villages and had their own Home Guards to protect them if the bandits went too far and were treated by the Malays almost as local folk heroes. The Malay Regiment stationed at the camp about six miles out of Mentakab had many battles with them and held their own. The local police had its lieutenants in the kampongs and their jungle squads had a series of running battles with the bandits and had almost a personal knowledge and understanding with them. As always, most of the security forces casualties were suffered in road ambushes. The Sultan of Pahang put on a brave face and sailed up and down the river on a regular basis, stopping at the kampongs to attend village dances. The river kampongs were relatively safe and the police and army had the situation fairly well covered.

The bandits and the security forces chased each other like cat and mouse and apart from some very serious ambushes with high casualties, you were reasonably safe if you kept your eyes well open. Now Tras, Benta, Bentong, Karak and Manchis were very dangerous places. They were on the main road between Kuala Lipis in the north and Mentakab further south. These areas were patrolled by at least two battalions of Gurkhas (1,500 men). It was reported that on one occasion the Gurkhas met a gang of 150 CTs, dropped their weapons and attacked the bandits with their kukris. Doubtless a few of them would have known that they had met the Gurkhas. There is no doubt that it was impossible to drive along the road from Karak to Manchis without being ambushed. The headquarters of the terrorist forces was probably in the area just west of Kampong Manchis and if you take a straight line to the west from Manchis over the Genting Peras the distance to Kuala Lumpur was only about 50 miles.

Police Lieutenant Barron was stationed at Mentakab and had been there for nearly a year when a young OCPD (Officer Commanding Police District) took over the district police station. I won't name him in case I embarrass him if he reads this book, but enough to say that he was a brave, clean-cut, good looking man with a friendly smile and dark brown curly hair. He was a "bit mad" (like we all were) but this Assistant Superintendent of Police would stand no nonsense from his lieutenants, on the other hand he was always ready to sit down with them and have a drink or two if asked. The police lieutenant had been out on patrol for about two months and the OCPD questioned him on his return as to where he had been and what he had been doing. "I've been killing bandits" said P/LT. Barron. The OCPD let him know in no uncertain manner that he didn't believe him. "You've probably been lazing around the kampongs eating well and seeing too much of the local women" he said. Barron didn't say much, grunted a little and within a few hours was out on another patrol. This time he was away about four weeks and came back with the same story. The OCPD said, "This is your last chance, Barron. If you let me down again you're on your way home." "Don't be long this time, Barron" said the OCPD, "and I want to see some results this time, or you're out". Two months went by and Barron returned. "That's it" said the OCPD, "Go down to the police lieutenants' mess, get your kit packed and be ready to go down to police headquarters in KL tomorrow morning. I'm sending them a signal now and you'll be straight on the plane home."

Barron turned to the OCPD and said "Wait a minute". He called over his shoulder, "Corporal" and into the office walked his Special Constable Jungle Squad Corporal and within a few seconds had tipped five CT heads on to the OCPD's desk. "Sort that lot out" said Barron and, without another word, left the office.

*   *   *   *   *   *

Temerloh was about five miles from Mentakab and as one of my jobs as OC Signals I had to visit the operator and radio at Kampong Chenor down the river. It only took a few minutes by land rover to Temerloh and very soon I was entering the back door of Temerloh Police Station. It didn't seem to have a front door. The police station seemed deserted except for the sound of two European voices shouting from one room to another. "Right, Tom" said one of the voices and, after a few minutes, it was "again". On further investigation, I found one of the voices. It was the Assistant OCPD and he was in the process of vigorously turning the handle of an army telephone. He did this several times, in fact every time the voice from the other room shouted "Again, Tom" he would turn the handle of the telephone. I was curious and followed the two wires leading from the telephone out through the door, down the corridor and into another room. There sat the OCPD Temerloh and sitting opposite him on a chair sat a very frightened looking captured bandit. To explain, the wires led from where Tom was turning the handle of the telephone to where in the other room sat the OCPD and the captured bandit. The bandit was made to hold the two wires, one in each hand and with an interpreter it was explained to him that he would be asked questions and if either he didn't answer or the answer was unsatisfactory, then a charge of electricity would be passed through his body from the two wires. It was further explained that each time the electricity was applied to him it would be stronger and stronger and that eventually it would be strong enough to kill him. The truth of the matter was that the voltage that turning the telephone handle produced was about 40 volts and was only capable of producing a mild shock. I didn't stay long for I didn't want to spoil their game, but I learned later that the bandit did give a lot of useful information as to where his 'friends' were and how many, etc. After arranging for some transport to take me to Kampong Chenor the following day, I left Temerloh and went back to Mentakab.

About six weeks before this there had been a particularly nasty ambush on the Chenor Road where 12 Malay police constables and special constables had been killed and so a journey to Chenor would mean at least three vehicles and an escort of about 15 men. We started off from Temerloh about ten o'clock on the following morning. The police escorts seemed very nervous but after crossing the Pahang River by ferry (the land rovers had to go up a ramp onto the ferry and down another ramp when we arrived at the other side) they seemed a little easier. The road was wet and slippery and nobody talked as we travelled the first five miles of the 12 mile journey. It was fairly open country but soon the road narrowed and the jungle closed in on our three land rovers. On we went at about 15 miles an hour. The jungle on our left fell away to deep ravines, whilst on the right there were steep banks covered with thick jungle foliage. One of the lads in the second land rover about ten yards behind us quietly started singing a current hit of the time called *The Laughing Samba*. The words went:

It's the laughing Samba
Something like a Rumba
It's the laughing Samba
Ha-ha-ha-ha-ha

It was now raining quite heavily and I thought I'd join the singing to cheer myself up. The double S bends where the previous ambush had happened was about 100 yards ahead. I took the bren machine gun from one of the escorts behind me and in a show of bravado pointed it continuously into the jungle on the right of the road. The rain continued, it was streaming down my face and I continued to sing louder and louder (probably in sheer terror). As we swung into and out of the bends everybody joined in the singing, especially the bit at the end ha-ha-ha-ha-ha. We must have looked and sounded a crazy bunch as we ploughed along. Anyway, we reached Chenor none the worse for wear and in high spirits. To continue on this crazy theme, the man in charge of Chenor Police Station was considered even by us to be a little eccentric in the tricks he used to pull. In truth, he was a charming man of about 28 years old and lived in Southend in England before he joined the Malay police as a Police Lieutenant.

He painted white skull and crossbones on the front of the hats of his jungle squad and swore that he had a standing arrangement with the local terrorists that when he was in Chenor, they stayed in the jungle and, when he went into the jungle with his squad, they moved into Chenor. He swore to me that he used the same coffee shop as they did. "What I do" explained Paul, "I make a lot of noise when I leave Chenor and I make a lot of noise when I come back. As I come in through one end of the kampong the terrorists leave at the other end". "It works well" said Paul, "the local Malay bandit leader and I have a good understanding with each other". To this day, I don't know whether he was telling the truth or not.

I knew that a local rubber planter had captured a terrorist on his estate near Mentakab. Apparently, the planter (a very pleasant Scotsman) was doing the rounds with just a pistol. He was accompanied by his Alsatian dog. The terrorist came towards the planter holding a hand grenade. The planter's Alsatian dog jumped at the terrorist and sank its teeth into his arm. The frightened CT dropped the grenade and fell over. The planter was able to point his pistol at the CT and bring him in to Mentakab Police Station. It was indeed a very brave act by both planter and dog. The following evening it was my turn to do the rounds of Mentakab; the banks, OSPC's (Officer Supervising Police Circle) house etc. One of the places I had to visit was Mentakab Hospital. The CT was sitting up in a small ward, smiling and looking very happy. The SC guard told me that he had been questioned by Special Branch during the day and given them some quite useful information. The CT had broken his right arm when he had fallen on the estate and the hospital had put the arm in Plaster of Paris so that it would heal. I think that the CT thought that all his troubles were over, but this was far from the truth. He was taken down to Pudu Jail in KL, put on trial about three days later and hung ten days after being captured. He was still in the plaster cast when he was hung, so it was reported.

*   *   *   *   *   *

Police Lieutenant James was in charge at Pesagi Police Station. Kampong Pesagi was on the banks of the Pahang River and it was the job of the police officer to defend the kampong and its inhabitants. Pesagi was just down the river from Chenor. Most nights the local CTs used to come down to the jungle edge and fire at the police station. It was not very pleasant for Pesagi James, as we used to call him, but he seemed to be standing up to it quite well and told us a few good tales when he came into Mentakab (usually about once every two or three weeks).

James had drunk a few bottles of beer and was thinking of going to bed. The firing from the jungle edge had eased off and James was feeling at peace with the world. The telephone rang, the SC said "It's General Templer". Pesagi roared with laughter and thought that it wasn't a good joke for this time of night. He picked up the telephone and a voice spoke, "This is General Templer here. I shall be in your area tomorrow and may call in to see you. I'll probably come by the river but nothing is fixed definite yet". "Oh, piss off" said Pesagi and put the telephone down. Early the following morning a telephone call from the OCPD at Mentakab ordered Police Lieutenant James to report to him immediately. On arriving at Mentakab he was told to go to police headquarters in KL and report. When he arrived in KL a senior police officer told him to report to King's House where the High Commissioner General Templer wanted to see him. Pesagi James, dressed in his best police uniform, stood waiting outside General Templer's office for about two hours. Eventually, he was summoned into the presence of General Templer who was busily working on some papers on his desk. He did not look up for about ten minutes and during this time James was standing stiffly to attention. Eventually, he looked up and said, "Are you Police Lieutenant James from Pesagi?" "Yes, Sir" said Pesagi, in a high-pitched croak. "Well, piss off then" said the General. Pesagi blinked, saluted, turned smartly about and scurried out. Whilst Templer was the best thing that ever happened to Malaya, his sense of justice could sometimes be quite crude. When we were told about this, we thought that General Templer had got it just right.

*　　*　　*　　*　　*　　*

One morning I was having a cup of tea in the OCPD's office at Mentakab Police Station. He was sitting in his chair behind his desk with his back to the window. I was standing on his right-hand side with my cup of tea on his desk. The OCPD wore two pistols (cowboy style), one on each side of his waist and when he left his office he always tucked a Gurkha kukri in his belt at the back. That was the OCPD ready for any emergency, a colourful sight. As I have said, he was well liked by the police lieutenants in Mentakab and to prove it that morning the Lieutenant i/c Special Constables Mentakab, appeared at the door and asked nonchalantly for a cup of tea.

The OCPD ignored him. "He's got a cup of tea. Where's mine?" The OCPD roared in a loud voice, "Get out of my office". The P/Lt. didn't move. "If you don't get out of my office by the time I count to five, I'll shoot you", the OCPD drew both his pistols and pointed them towards the police lieutenant. "One, two, three," he counted and the P/Lt.'s face turned pale. The thought that the OCPD had finally "flipped his lid" crossed his mind and he turned round to get out of the office. "Four, five" shouted the boss. Two pistol shots rang out almost together. The OCPD had raised both his pistols over his head, stretched backwards in his chair and fired them out of the window. You couldn't get to the back of the office and so it was quite safe. The P/Lt., still looking distinctly shaken, walked into the office and said to the OCPD, "You're a stupid bastard". The OCPD laughed and shrugged his shoulders. The place took you like that sometimes and you had to be a bit crazy to survive.

*   *   *   *   *   *

About four hundred men had come out to Malaya in response to newspaper advertisements in British newspapers. They were a mixed bunch, but you wouldn't find better anywhere in the world. They were wild when they were relaxing and calm when in danger and, like the Malay Special Constables they commanded, they had a lot of patience. Many were to lose their lives in the fight for Malaya's freedom, but the police lieutenants made sure that they never had a dull moment by working hard and playing hard. The average police lieutenant was usually given the name of a kampong or even just a map reference and told to go there, recruit the local Malays as Special Constables and then go out into the jungle and kill terrorists. A tall order when you can't speak a word of the language and have only a limited knowledge of firearms and the local terrain. In spite of these odds, they achieved considerable success. This success could not have been achieved without the Special Constables (they were mostly Malays, with some Indians, and a few Chinese).

The SCs as they were always called, were the most overworked, underpaid, undervalued and unappreciated group of fighters during the Emergency.

Every rubber plantation, tin mine and public building had to be guarded and protected against attack. They had to be guarded 24 hours every day, seven days a week and 52 weeks every year. The Special Constables usually lived in squalid conditions at the back of a building or in poorly-built small quarters. As guards they could easily be observed during the day and this information was passed by the Min Yuen to the active service units of the CTs. There were about 50,000 SCs and more than 2,000 of them were killed. They shouldered this responsibility with honour, but I'm sure that the indifference shown to them by senior police officers hurt them a lot. They were, in my opinion, the largest single factor which enabled the Emergency to be fought. They formed the backbone of the jungle squads that the police lieutenants took out into the jungle and the P/Lt.s depended on them by night and day during those cruel times. The police lieutenants lost 150 killed out of 400 of that rank. It was a very dodgy job, 25,000 regular police, 30,000 British troops, 10,000 Gurkhas and eventually 200,000 Home Guards.

Of course, the deciding factor was the way General Templer inspired everyone and planned an efficient counter-attack against the terrorists. Within four weeks of taking over as High Commissioner he had constructed and issued form Z.Z. This was a questionnaire which had to be answered every week by all police and army units. It asked such things as, when did you last contact CTs, how many were in your party, how were you armed, what time of day was it, did you act on information, and the final question was "Being wise after the event, what could you have done to have obtained better results?". After we had laboriously filled in the forms every week for about three months, Templer analysed the results. A few of his conclusions led to direct orders to us such as, only take out patrols when you have good information, ambushing food dumps can be useful, always set up your ambushes just inside the jungle edge, not in the rubber trees, no routine patrolling in the future, the best time to operate, the best number to take on patrol and how they should be armed, etc. It worked, and very soon we were getting better results.

OCPD Mentakab and a police lieutenant fixing the fire extinguishers at Mentakab Police Station.

4. The Chinese

Before the Emergency, the Chinese had played a major role in the economy and commerce of Malaya and the situation had been much the same since the early days of the British rule. It is true to say that the British held the government posts and the rubber estates and the tin mines were owned and controlled by them, but apart from that, the Chinese owned and controlled everything. Shops, restaurants, food markets and many banks, transport systems and insurance organisations were all controlled by the Chinese. The only commercial enterprise that they didn't control were the railways which were run by the Indians. The Indians had run them well whilst they were in India and they continued to run them well in Malaya. When the Emergency ended in the early 1960s, the Malays took over government with a very firm hand and Chinese influence in commerce and industry rapidly declined. Most private concerns which had previously been owned by Chinese were gradually shifted over to Malay control and if you go into a fairly large department store nowadays in KL you will find at least three or four Malay women and girls behind every counter and the main offices such as the police department, the army, the post office, the main public buildings, tourist centres are all staffed by Malay men and women. It is not the same without the Chinese, and I must admit that rogues though some of them are, I am sorry to see their faces almost disappear from the commerce of Malaysia. They can still be seen on the outskirts of most towns, their communities are still intact and some of their numbers who remained loyal to the government during the Emergency have held and are still holding the highest positions in the

Malaysian government's administration. Communism ruined the lives of practically the whole of the Chinese population of Malaya (pardon me if I keep calling it Malaya), what would you have done, give some Chinese half-starved bandit a handful of rice or chance getting your throat cut? They did their best to keep out of the Emergency for the sake of their family's safety and their own safety, but many were drawn in to it, as we have said, whether they wanted to or not. Many remained neutral but the Min Yuen were always listening. Most people in the world put self-preservation at the top of their list of priorities and the Chinese are no exception to this. Now that Communism is out of fashion, perhaps the Malaysian government will be a little more tolerant with the Chinese. I am sure that they value the help which many Chinese could give them but they have to be constantly wary that other racial factions do not start any trouble. It is easy to criticise the Malaysian government on this issue, but they must tread "softly, softly" and the situation must be very tactfully handled. They should, as Templer said, "find their solutions in the hearts and minds of the people" *(Lieutenant-General Sir Gerald Templer, 1952)*.

But to consider the Emergency again, if the Chinese terrorists had lost the battle, which they did, they were free to go back to China, but you will note that very few of them did. On the other hand, if the Malays had lost where could they have run to – nowhere!

There was, as we had previously said, a hard-core of MPAJA (Malayan People's Anti-Japanese Army) left in the jungle in the early 1950s. Their allegiance to the Malayan Communist Party had not changed and their objective (to take over the government of Malaya) remained the same. I have a feeling that though the Chinese all originally came into Malaya from China and most people immediately lumped them in with the Chinese mainland, I strongly feel that the Chinese in Malaya did not want to go back there. They had come to Malaya full of hope for the future in this land of plenty and I feel that given the situation they would have jealously guarded their independence from other Communist influences in the world. My limited knowledge of the Chinese tells me that they do not want to be Communists, not any of them. They are natural entrepreneurs and will work night and day to see their family business prosper. This is not Communism, this is Capitalism. As the gamblers we know they are, they thrive on taking business chances. Look across the Causeway to Singapore and you will see a prosperous community working well together and doing very well, thank you. More than fifty percent of them are Chinese and they play a leading part in the continued success of the island. The first step for the hard core leadership to take was to recruit more bandits and more Min Yuen. Get them into the fight was the message, recruit, recruit, recruit, that was what they did from Johor in the south to Kedah and Kelantan in the north. At least six new regiments of terrorists had to be trained and the offensive was to begin on a massive scale. That was 1950 and it was not a very good year for the people of Malaya and its security forces. By the end of that year they were facing at least five thousand armed terrorists and countless thousands of their helpers, some of whom carried arms, even if it was only a pistol.

The largest regiment headquarters were in Pahang near to Kampong Manchis, in Perak near Tapah and in Johor near Kluang. Some of these large camps could hold up to 200 terrorists, and gangs of up to 150 bandits roaming around doing their mischief was not uncommon, especially in Pahang where, on several occasions, they took over small towns and held on to them for several days.

The bandit gangs were made up of a cross-section of the Chinese community, some very bright and some not so bright, but they were all dedicated to the cause of Communism. They took chances that many others would not have taken. Their camps were well concealed and their huts were built of bamboo frames, bound together with rattan which is a vine that hangs down from the canopy of the jungle, and they were covered with attap leaves which are surprisingly waterproof if they are woven together in the correct way. They had to be near a fresh water supply (usually a stream) and not too far away from the local inhabitants who could help them to obtain food supplies. They did grow some vegetables near the camp but as signs of cultivation were easily spotted from the air, they had to limit this type of food supply. The terrorists had to abide by a few golden rules if they were to survive in these camps. Firstly, they had to have sentries posted at the possible entries to the camp for twenty four hours a day. If the camp was being attacked or looked likely to be attacked, then the sentry would fire a warning shot to warn his comrades. Most sentries and most leading scouts on bandit patrols carried sawn-off shot guns for they were very effective and made a very big bang. Secondly, there had to be a pre-arranged escape route from the camp which gave them the safest method of escape. Thirdly, each member of the gang had to be fully packed and ready to leave immediately at a few minutes' notice and they must all know where they were to reassemble and at what time (approximately). This was very important and for sure if they did not arrange this place and turn up at the appointed time they might never see each other again. Visibility in deep jungle is only two or three yards, so you can imagine that they were most unlikely to find each other again.

Most camps which the security forces attacked were empty when they arrived on the scene, but showed signs of occupation in the very recent past. Discipline in the camps was very strict and fraternising with female bandits was strictly forbidden. Every camp in the country had a strict routine each day which was followed without fail, unless they were involved with anti-security force operations.

The Manchis terrorists were mostly Hakkas and the girls took the same risks every day as the men. They carried the same loads and were treated by the leadership in exactly the same way. The routine was: –

4.30 am	Food supply foragers and messengers leave the camp after a very small meal had been taken.
5.30 am	Roll-call followed by early morning PT which was usually running around the camp (in the dark) shouting numbers at the tops of their voices. A strange way of starting the day.
6.00 am	Washing their bodies and faces and cleaning their teeth (the Chinese are a very clean people and great care was taken over this).
6.30 am	It was now light and they had a parade when they sang "The Red Flag" and saluted the Communist flag, followed by a propaganda talk by the patrol leader. The girls were neatly dressed in black trousers and long-sleeved blouses.
7.00 am	Cleaning weapons and weapons drill. The terrorists were very poor shots and most of their arms and ammunition were in a very poor state of preservation. As you can imagine, the damp jungle atmosphere quickly rusts steel and they had to keep both their arms and their ammunition well oiled.
9.00 am	Breakfast – a meal of boiled tapioca and rice, a selection of vegetables and this was followed by a hot drink which was usually just hot water.
9.30 am	Everyone had to learn to read and write Mandarin (the national language of China) and this was usually taught by one of the better-educated girls.
12.00 noon	Most of the afternoon was taken up by lectures and discussions organised by the patrol leaders.

4.00 pm	The main meal was taken. This was the usual rice and vegetables and if the supplies were good, there was sometimes some dried fish or some other delicacy.
5.00 pm	Again, general discussions – this monotonous routine could not have been endured by any race except the Chinese, for they are a gregarious people who like to hear themselves and other people talking. Sanity prevailed for six days and Sunday was a day off.

As we have said, life was very difficult for the Chinese because they were between two fires. The first breakthrough probably came when the size of the Home Guard was increased and everyone who joined was issued with a single-barrelled shotgun. The Chinese joined the Home Guard in large numbers, for at last they could now protect themselves and their families against any acts of vengeance by the Communists.

In 1950 and 1951 many well-educated Chinese youths of about eighteen years of age joined the police as recruit Signallers and trained up into excellent wireless operators.

On Saturday, the 6th of October, 1951, at Fraser's Hill, the High Commissioner, Sir Henry Gurney, was attacked and killed by a strong force of bandits. They were ambushed on the pass and that ambush was supervised by Sui Mah, the Commander of the 11th Regiment. The High Commissioner's Rolls Royce car had thirty five bullet holes in it which gives an indication of the ferocity of the ambush.

During 1951 five hundred and thirty two civilians were killed and also five hundred and five security force members.

But would the tide turn, we hoped so and when Sir Winston Churchill appointed Sir Gerald Templer as High Commissioner in February, 1952, we kept our fingers crossed.

5. General Templer

Lieutenant-General Sir Gerald Templer was appointed as High Commissioner and arrived in Malaya in February 1952. Templer was faced with the primary task of defeating the Communist Terrorists.

Here at last we had a brilliant man who understood people. He was the "salt of the earth" and knew all the swear words. He was able to understand most of what was going on almost instantly and most important of all he knew what to do to solve the problems. This was his greatest talent. Trained at the Royal Military College of Sandhurst in England he became, during the Second World War, the youngest man to reach the rank of Lieutenant-General. He was an excellent soldier and certainly believed in the old adage that "time spent in reconnaissance is time never wasted", proving it by his excellent use of the police "Special Branch" during his first two years. He was fifty four when he took on the onerous task of fighting the Malayan Communist Terrorists.

Templer wanted to know what was happening in the country and so he went everywhere and spoke to anybody and everybody. Reports from other people were no good to him, he must go and see for himself and that is exactly what he did. Sometimes Templer made instant decisions and issued instant orders, usually with a time proviso, for example he would say to the District Officer accompanying him, "I want a school building here and I'll give you four weeks to get it built". If the District Officer did not carry out the order, he was dismissed and put on the next boat home. Templer was not interested in excuses and "red tape", he wanted his orders carried out and the word soon got out that he was not a man to be trifled with.

He was tall and slim with moods that could change like tropical weather can change from bright sunshine one moment to torrents of rain the next. He had a wonderful wife with him called Jane and an equally beautiful teenage daughter. They were a great help to him in his work and gave a lot of their time to the Red Cross and the hospitals. They certainly gave emphasis to the saying that "behind every successful man there is a good woman". Everyone knew that General Templer would stand no nonsense, but it was proved beyond all shadow of doubt by the action he took at Tanjong Malim, a small town of some 20,000 people about 50 miles north of Kuala Lumpur. The Gordon Highlanders (a British army regiment) had just lost seven men killed in a terrorist ambush in the area when the next incident occurred. Early one morning in March a group of workmen were being escorted by a police patrol so that they could repair the water pipe line that had been cut by the bandits. They were ambushed by more than 40 CTs and eleven members of the patrol were killed including the Assistant District Officer. The terrorists took the arms from the dead policemen and vanished into the surrounding jungle. After the burial of the casualties, Templer descended on the town and spoke to the town's leaders. He was in cold fury as he spoke and after telling them they were responsible for the ambush, that they were cowards and traitors, he announced his punishment on the town.

All shops and schools would close, the buses would not run, no one would leave or enter the town and there would be a curfew of 22 hours out of every 24 hours every day until further notice. Their rice ration would also be halved, said Templer. This meant that the adult rice ration was reduced from five katis per head per week to three katis.

He then arranged for a letter and questionnaire to be delivered by British troops to every home in the town and ordered people to put their forms into boxes whether they had answered the questions or not and the boxes were then sealed and taken by the troops down to King's House in Kuala Lumpur. Representatives of the local community also went with the forms and watched General Templer look at each form, make notes from them where necessary and then destroy them in front of the representatives. A few days later, a second batch of forms were delivered and the same procedure followed.

Two days later, Special Branch made the first of 35 arrests and the curfew was lifted. Shortly afterwards, 3,500 Chinese volunteered for the Home Guard, were issued with their shotguns and from that point onwards Tanjong Malim became one of the most peaceful areas in the country.

Another example of the way Templer worked with Special Branch was of course his famous form ZZ. It really was a "market research" and asked all the pertinent questions about police and army contacts with the terrorists. The answers to the questions were analysed by the General, like he had done at Tanjong Malim and then action was taken. This was Templer putting theory into practice and it worked out very well.

Another stroke of genius was the way he developed the reward system leading to the capture or killing of terrorists. The rewards ranged from 2,500 Malayan dollars for a rank and file bandit to 100,000 dollars for the top man. Rewards were also given to terrorists who surrendered, or to people who helped them to surrender.

That's how Templer carried on from start to finish, brutally honest, but very fair, one in a million and perhaps the only one who could have done the job. Full marks to Churchill for putting him on the job. Templer gave his all for his country and Malaysia should always be grateful to the man who helped to save them from the wicked chains of Communism.

General Templer meeting some `scouts' in Kuala Lumpur.

6. The Gurkhas

Today there are eleven Gurkha Infantry regiments in operation. Unfortunately they are in constant threat of being reduced in numbers, due to the economic pressures being applied by the British and Indian Governments.

The Gurkha is affectionately known to the British soldier as "Johnny Gurkha". The battle cry of the Gurkhas is "Ayo Gurkhali" which in English means "the Gurkhas are upon you".

They are brave, honest and full of confidence. They rarely lie or steal and would rather die in battle than turn and run from the enemy.

There is no record of a Gurkha ever being court-martialled or being found guilty of desertion and army records show no evidence of a Gurkha ever being flogged.

They are about five feet six inches tall, swarthy in complexion and, have almond-shaped eyes and high cheekbones. Their hair is black and quite thick. Their staple diet is curry and rice, washed down with many pints of hot, sweet, milky tea. They have strong thigh and calf muscles, developed in the hills of Nepal by carrying heavy loads over long distances.

When they have passed their basic training they each take an oath, which they swear on their kukris. They "eat the salt" (literally) and swear never to break their oath which is that they would rather die than behave in a dishonourable way.

Gurkhas have a very good sense of humour, they do not boast, and they also have very shy personal habits.

They come from the hills of Nepal which is a small country to the north of India and about the size of England. Most of them come from four main tribes, the Magars, the Gurungs, the Limbus, and the Rais. The British army invaded Nepal in the early 1800s and suffered heavy casualties at the hands of the Gurkhas. After the short war, the British and Gurkhas found out that they had a mutual respect for each other and eventually they were recruited into the British army about the year 1815.

It is curious but some enemies have an almost warm respect for each other. Front-line British troops found that out during both world wars against the Germans, that respect existed on both sides. Never mind what the mindless wonders of government office tell you, or the newspapers.

If you want to instil discipline and hand out punishments to most soldiers in the world you would probably follow the following procedure.

(a) Set some basic rules and lay down a list of punishments for disobeying those rules.
(b) Train them to fight efficiently.

Most soldiers in the world will obey orders, some more willingly than others and very many would grumble about the orders they were given. The Gurkhas are different, they obey orders instantly and carry them out with cheerful efficiency.

Punishment for most soldiers means being confined to barracks, extra guard duties and extra drill parades. Again, the Gurkhas are different. To punish a Gurkha you would compel him to leave the barracks or stop him doing guard duties or not allow him to take part in drill parades.

To give you an idea of the confidence that the Gurkha officers had in their men, here follows an account. The Colonel of the battalion that was with us (1st/2nd) was making a habit of disappearing for two or three days, so much so that the Intelligence Officer of the battalion plucked up enough courage to ask him where he had been. The Colonel snapped, "I've been going out into the Ulu (jungle) with two or three of my Gurkhas to have a look around. Don't worry about me, I'm always safe when I'm with two or three of my Gurkhas".

It would appear that he would take a few of the Intelligence section with him and then, armed with just his walking stick and presumably his personal pistol, would go on "picnics" in the jungle. We didn't see much of the 1st/2nd at headquarters, perhaps just a few orderlies and some base-employed officers. The system they used was to set up a base camp in deep jungle and work from there. They would pick an area of jungle that had plenty of terrorists in it, and after some thought, set up camp right in the middle of it. Then they would "fan out" daily, patrolling and ambushing until they had rid the area of the terrorists.

We would just be told that a section had successfully contacted bandits at a particular grid (map) reference and that the bodies of the dead terrorists were being unloaded from their vehicles in front of the police station. We then had to find out what had happened and who the dead terrorists were.

One day, five khaki hats complete with red stars and peaks were delivered to us in the "Ops. Room" with the Company Commander's compliments, of course. The story ran that a section of the 1st/2nd had come across five terrorists who had stopped for a rest and were sitting on a log. The Gurkhas attacked and the bandits ran, they ran so fast that they did not have time to put on their hats. Apart from the one at the back, who the Gurkhas killed, they all escaped. One could almost imagine the scene which I have always thought a cartoonist would have had a "field day" with. I always ima-gined the picture would show five bandits running very fast, with the Gurkhas in hot pursuit. The bandit hats, I always imagined, would be in the air above the bandits, motionless, as if suspended in a time capsule.

*   *   *   *   *   *

I was invited by the police lieutenant stationed at North Hummock Estate to go with him to the Gurkha base camp, not far from North Hummock. Like a fool, I said yes and very soon we were on our way. There were two police lieutenants and a Special Constable driver. The driver put his foot down for obvious reasons and I'm sure that during the journey we spent more time in the air than on the track. We would hit a bump at about sixty miles an hour, take off several feet into the air and then land again, hit another bump, take off and so we continued until we reached the camp.

The camp itself was very quiet, doubtless most men would be either out on patrol or sleeping. We stayed in the officers' mess tent for about an hour chatting about nothing in particular but the officer who was entertaining us kept slipping us glasses of rum. Just have one more before you go back, he kept saying with a cheery smile. It was very sweet and seemed a little thicker in consistency than shop rum. The journey back to the estate, I don't remember it at all. If we are talking about soldiers, then the Gurkha is probably the best "attack" soldier of them all. They are fearless and the British have been proud to have been associated with them for the past two hundred years.

During the time they were in action in Malaya (1948–1959) they killed more than one thousand five hundred Communist terrorists. Their own number killed was fifty nine. The 2nd/6th battalion suffered the first casualty in July 1948 when one of its platoons was ambushed by Liew Kon Kim and his Number One Platoon in the Kajang area of Selangor. After retraining the 2nd/6th stayed in the Kluang area of Johor for nearly three years and in that time they killed more than eighty terrorists.

Here are a few exploits which will give you some idea of the contacts a number of the battalions had.

1st/6th Gurkha Rifles

In January 1949, a platoon of "A" Company was ambushed by

Gurkhas on jungle patrol

Gurkhas on jungle patrol

terrorists. It happened in Sintok, north of Alor Star which is very close to the Thailand border. Two officers, one British and one Gurkha were killed as well as nine Gurkha soldiers. The officers who were at the front with the leading section were killed with the first bursts of terrorist fire. The platoon fired back at the terrorists and because the ambush was so tight and well prepared they found themselves unable to fight back effectively. They were forced to withdraw taking their eleven dead with them.

1st/6th Gurkha Rifles

On the 10th of March, 1949, a gang of more than one hundred and fifty CTs were reported in the Jerantut area of Pahang. The Gurkhas followed up the gang and the footprints showed that the terrorists were several hours ahead of them. On the following morning, the tracks were again followed and within two hours they ran into the sentry of a large bandit camp. There were about thirty huts in the camp and several bursts of fire were exchanged. The camp was in thick jungle and it had dense thorns down one side of it.

In six attacks during the next three days the Gurkhas killed six CTs, but investigation of the area at a later date concluded that many more had been killed and carried away by their comrades. The chase and the battles went on for five days. Gurkha casualties were fortunately nil.

1st/2nd Gurkha Rifles

On the 22nd of January, 1950, in the Jabis area of Johor, two platoons of Gurkhas contacted CTs in the early hours of the morning. The leading Gurkha killed four terrorists during his first two bursts of fire. The Company Commander (a British Major) killed two terrorists and then saw another CT slashing at a Gurkha with a parang (a large knife). The Gurkha was badly cut about the head and neck and died in hospital a few hours later. One of the platoons outflanked the main party of terrorists (encircled them from one side) and after the battle twelve terrorist bodies were recovered. A few months later, it was established that probably more than thirty five CTs had been killed in that action.

2/7th Gurkha Rifles

On the 11th of August, 1951, at Saroi (near Seremban in Selangor), the Gurkhas were ambushed by about sixty CTs. The wireless operator managed to get a message through to the Company Commander at headquarters. He asked for help. The Gurkhas had by now almost used up all of their ammunition and were preparing for an attack with just their kukris. I have spoken to this Company Commander recently and he told me that with shouts of "Ayo Gurkhali", the relief group of about twenty rushed forward and were able to put the bandits to flight and also they were able to kill about eight terrorists at the same time.

1st/10th Gurkha Rifles

We will consider the magnificient work done by this battalion later in the book when we talk about a town in Pahang called Bentong. Bentong, Karak and Manchis were amongst the worst areas for bandit attrocities in those times and when the battalion left Bentong, the people of the town presented them with the following letter.

To

The Commanding Officer
Officers and men
The 1st/10th Gurkha Rifles

Sir,

Your battalion arrived in Pahang over a year ago when spirits were low; we need not remind you of those days of terror, murders and ambushes which took their dreadful toll on all nationalities. Through the skill and energies of your men, the district has improved beyond all recognition. The name of the battalion has struck fear into the hearts of the bandits, many of whom have fallen to your guns. It would be foolish to say that the district has been entirely cleaned up, for much remains to be done, but during your stay you have achieved one of the most important things, you have won the complete confidence of the people. Never before, we believe, has so mixed a community taken a battalion to its hearts so readily. The battalion has been integrated with the civil population quite spontaneously at all levels. There has never been the slightest friction. Nothing but continued displays of mutual trust. We are grateful to you. We shall never forget you. We know that our sincere and lasting gratitude will be some consolation.

Signed by the leaders of the Chinese, Malay,Indian and Ceylonese people of Bentong, 25th Februrary 1952

*   *   *   *   *   *

Gurkha rations contain the makings of a curry they call "Bhat". When eaten with vegetables and rice, it makes a substantial meal. Washed down with hot, sweet milky tea, of course. It was usually cooked over a "Tommy cooker" which is solid paraffin wax and will burn hot in most weather conditions. The last drink of the day which the Gurkha has usually contains a good "tot" of rum.

If you are lucky enough to go into action with them as a soldier, you will feel as happy as a young child holding his mother's hand or a baby being breast fed. Do not worry about your skin, let them take care of it for you. If the enemy dare to present themselves, they are usually attacked immediately and the Gurkhas usually come out on top.

Even though some eight or nine battalions were available for the Emergency, this was just a paper figure, for on the ground when you consider the retraining and refitting they had to do, they were lucky to put out 3,000 men. Not a lot you may say, but when you consider who they were, they were sufficient to cope with any situation, and they did.

7. Joining and the Early Days

Our first point of contact with the police was in the Navy petty officers' mess at HMS Terror in Singapore. Our batch of about 12 men were issued with police uniform, a 9mm Browning revolver and a small cardboard box containing 48 rounds of ammunition. One recruit who was with us there was undoubtedly an ex-public school boy who kept announcing to us all that he had not had a letter yet from his mummy and that he was very worried about this. He caused us not a little amusement and we all thought that here was one who would be "easy meat" for the terrorists. A pep talk from a serving officer advised us to always keep the last bullet to shoot ourselves and that if we couldn't carry the terrorist bodies out of the jungle, the thing to do was to cut off either their heads or fingers for identification purposes. We thought that he was obviously deranged but one of our number, a tough-looking ex-London Bobby said he'd heard enough and asked to be sent home straight away. I think that his request was granted. Bandits, terrorists, who were these people, were they as dangerous as the police officer had implied, or was it just his idea of a joke? We heard, probably just rumours, we hoped, that the night train from Singapore to Kuala Lumpur was ambushed two or three nights a week. As we boarded the train, we noticed two or three crash wagons on the line in front of the engine and machine guns mounted above the driver's cab. Maybe there was some truth in the rumours, after all. There were two of us in the sleeping compartment with upper and lower berths and because the journey of some 250 miles would take us most of the night, we settled down in uneasy comfort. The train stopped with a jolt, people were shouting and there were shadows rushing past the window.

'Kluang, Kluang', they were shouting and I noticed a few oriental faces looking through the window, but within a few minutes the train again jolted its way towards KL. Two hours or so later, the train stopped suddenly again, 'Segamat, Segamat', they were shouting, surely this was it, we couldn't get away with it again, but we did and two weary new police lieutenants arrived in KL exactly on time, 8am. Kluang, Segamat, had only been the names of railway stations where passengers had been getting on and off the train during the night, but we didn't know this at the time.

We thought we had survived a hair-raising adventure and our weak knees told the story as we stumbled towards the waiting police vehicle. A cheerful, too cheerful, we thought, young man dressed in shorts, tee shirt and sandals met us and said we were going to the police lieutenants' mess at Hose Road. Five minutes later we were there, unloaded our kit and given a room to share. "Members are requested to remain seated whilst the bar is in motion", read the sign above the bar. You turned left as you went in the door, there were about eight tables for eating on the left and at the far end was the focal point, the bar. Scattered around, in between the door and the bar were a dozen or so tables, each surrounded by four or five comfortable cane chairs with cushions on them, very nice indeed. A memorial plaque on the right hand wall with some 25 names on it reminded me that there was more to this job than was obvious. Wong and his family who lived in rooms at the back of the bar, looked after us. He was a gem and organised food, laundry, room cleaning, etc., his best act was the curry tiffin he prepared every Sunday lunch-time. The tables were set out like a first class restaurant and at about 12.15 pm with about 20 police lieutenants waiting hungrily at the table, he ceremoniously served the curried chicken (Malay style) with all the accompanying side dishes such as chutney, peanuts, chopped tomato, chopped onions, banana, etc. After the curry he served Gula Melaka, which is sago pudding covered with a thin treacle sauce made from brown sugar, never a great favourite, but who would offend Wong by refusing it? We certainly wouldn't. It was about five o'clock on the day I arrived at the mess and having been up for most of the previous night, as you will recall, I thought I would lie down on my bed in the room, stretch my legs and close my eyes. Tucking the mosquito net in around me, I relaxed. Suddenly hundreds of small flying creatures with flapping wings began to swarm around the room. They looked quite terrifying and I was worried in case they got under the mosquito net. I wondered, as I lay there frightened out of my wits, did these flying insects pack a deadly sting? I certainly didn't intend to come out from under the net to find out. From outside the room on the wooden verandah a Scotch voice boomed, "Which silly bastard left the light on in my room?" It was Jock Doyle, who was the roommate I had not yet met. As he switched off the lights in our room he explained to me that the creatures were flying ants, quite harmless and that they had been attracted by the light in the room. When the light went off they disappeared as quickly as they had arrived.

Jock was a very likeable man, very tough and he had done a bit of boxing. "I'll show you around KL after tea" said Jock. Soon after, his motor cycle was speeding down Hose Road and I was hanging on at the back. First it was the Coliseum on Batu Road where they have the biggest mixed grill in town, served on large oval plates and all for $3.50. Then to Nanto's Bar across the road where the main attractions were the three pretty Chinese girls behind the bar and a choice of Anchor Beer or Tiger Beer. Drinking an ice cold Anchor Beer when the sun is setting in the tropics is the nearest thing to paradise. After that it was back to Hose Road and bed. The fireflies gleamed their intermittent lights as they flew their merry way in the darkness and the world stood silently still before sleep ended that first exciting day.

"You wanna dance five dollar" said the "taxi" dancing girl. It was a good system and it worked well. There is no doubt in my mind that the Bukit Bintang Cabaret on Bukit Bintang Road in KL was good value for money. It was a very large dance hall with girls sitting in pairs separated by small tables on which they placed their cold soft drinks. Indian girls, Malay girls, Eurasian girls, almost every kind of girl you could imagine was there. You buy a book of three tickets for five dollars and when you want the girl to sit with you at a table for an hour that will be twelve dollars. A big band of good musicians, beautiful girls and a drink of beer, what more could a man ask for? You could try asking for more but you wouldn't get it. As we danced, Ruby cooed in my ear the old song, "They try to tell us we're too young". Ruby was pretty and if I could afford it when I went to the BB, I always booked her out. She was slim and of medium height, a good dancer and could chat all your worries away.

Of course, there was always the Eastern or the Lucky World Cabaret just past Campbell Road but Ruby wouldn't be there and though they were worth an occasional visit it was the BB for me nine times out of ten.

I had a spell at the police depot on Rifle Range Road which was on the northeast side of Kuala Lumpur, probably about four months in total. My job was to teach the police radio operators a little about the theory of radio. The recruit Signallers were a good bunch, a mixture of Malay and Indian mostly with a few Chinese which was the normal security force make-up. They were standard VII "boys" that's about 'O' level standard in the British system of education. Their English was excellent, both written and spoken.

Jock, as you will remember, was the police lieutenant I shared a room with at Hose Road, also ran the Police Operators Training School. Apart from general supervision, he taught radio telegraphy or the morse code to put it simply. The operators had to pass out at 18 words per minute and most of them did. Jock did very well in the police and was gazetted as a superintendent and eventually made the rank of Chief Superintendent. He deserved to do well for he worked hard at the job and turned out thousands of very good police wireless operators. These operators were then posted to remote police stations and would sometimes be sending and receiving as many as 3,000 groups (words) every morning in morse code. Most of it was the daily SITREP or situation report which told police and army commanders exactly what was happening in their area and other items which would be useful to them. After the four months or so at the depot (quite a cushy number), they told me I was posted to central Pahang as O/C Signals. They said that the convoy which usually came in from Mentakab on the Friday would pick me up at the mess on the Monday morning. A three ton truck arrived driven by a Police Lieutenant Barton. He was of average height and chubby, with a face that always wore a half smile which frequently would burst into a grin and then a loud chuckling laugh. As I was to find out later, Doug Barton was not easily frightened. We joined an armoured car and two land rovers in front of the Treasury Government building which was in front of the main Padang in the centre of KL and very soon we were on our way to Pahang.

Straight up Batu Road, take the Batu caves signs and then start climbing the steep, winding Genting Simpang which rises to about 4,000 feet. The road was very dangerous, not only because of possible ambushes but because of its geography. It was steep and on one side of it there was a drop of about 200 feet into thick jungle and on the other side high banks covered with thick vegetation held terror at every bend. One careless move on the part of the driver and you could easily finish up at the bottom of a jungle hole. Also, you couldn't afford to travel slowly up the Genting hill. Slow moving vehicles made an easier target and as our tactic was to drive through ambushes, speed was important. We reached the top of the hill after about an hour and stopped on Barton's signal.

A young man dressed in jungle green stepped out of the undergrowth. He was obviously very pleased to see us and Doug and the other two police lieutenants that were with us and they were soon talking with him in an animated way, interrupted by occasional bursts of uncontrollable laughter.

It was a morale raising exercise for the Genting lieutenant who controlled hundreds of square miles of "Sakai country" and led a very lonely life. The Sakai are the aborigines of Malaya and there are many thousands of them, mostly in the north of Malaya in the states of Pahang, Kelantan and Kedah. They still stalk their prey, usually small animals and monkey, with poison darts and blowpipes, to support their tapioca and fruit diet. The latter, they find in the jungle. When the game runs short in the area they move on, erect temporary long houses or huts and start hunting again. We usually saw some of them on this journey, in single file, trooping along the side of the road wearing next to nothing. The drive downhill was easier, another 20 or 30 miles, turn left at Kampong Gentong (there was a very good curry shop at that corner) and you arrived in Bentong some three or four minutes later. Here Doug had a contact, in fact Doug's best friend, with a cheerful smile and a mop of curly hair. They chatted away like long-lost brothers in the MT (Motor Transport) park outside the police station and they were obviously reluctant to part when we were ready to continue our journey.

*   *   *   *   *   *

The police station at Bentong was a gloomy, depressing place and on investigation, once you had passed through the front office charge room, you were confronted with an open area with six or eight large barred police cells on three sides of the square. The cells were crammed full of suspected terrorists, mostly Chinese, who had been picked up by the Gurkhas or the police doing their difficult work around Bentong.

The look of hate on all their faces was proof of guilt without examining any of their case histories. I hurried across the quadrangle and spent five or ten minutes talking to the police wireless operator. He was a carefree, cheerful Malay who did a good job daily keeping in contact with HQ at Lipis and seemed unaffected by the fearsome array of faces peering through the bars just outside his radio room. Bentong was a bad area and the Gurkhas had two companies there. There was also one company of British troops. Most of the British troops were national servicemen who were between 18 and 20 years old and had been conscripted to fight. They didn't like the life a lot and most of them were just looking forward to finishing their two years "national service". The Gurkhas were very different. They were professional soldiers who loved a fight, no matter what the odds. Each Gurkha carried his normal rifle or machine gun but his favourite weapon was his kukri which was tucked into the back of his belt. The kukri was 15 inches long with a wooden handle. The blade which had a broad back was curved and very sharp. It was well known that on many occasions the Gurkhas had discarded the weapons, drawn their kukris and with bloodthirsty screams, had attacked their enemies. Doubtless, the terrorists in the Bentong area were very frightened of them.

It was about 30 miles from Bentong to Mentakab but we had to go through Karak which was "real bandit country" so Doug explained. When we had completed about half of the journey, Doug suggested I take my lieutenant stars out of my shoulder epaulets. "No sense in advertising" he said with a smile. I took my stars out but felt embarrassed about it. We passed four Malays on the right of the road and then Semantan Estate before entering the town of Mentakab about 3 in the afternoon.

We swung into Doug's MT yard just across the Padang from the police station. "Hang on a minute" he said, disappeared into his office and then came out again and organised my kit to be taken out of the back of the truck and loaded into a land rover. He then ran me to the police lieutenants' mess.

"That's our mess there" said Doug, pointing to a Chinese coffee house on the corner, "We're above the coffee house". I heaved my kit and a suitcase up the steep stairs as he explained, "It used to be a brothel when the Japanese were here". Japanese brothel it may have been, but now it was home for seven or eight police lieutenants who slept in the rooms upstairs and ate their meals in the coffee shop downstairs.

There were two British army units stationed in Mentakab, a Royal Electrical and Mechanical Engineers unit (REME) just on the right as you entered the town, mostly used for repairing the motor vehicles of nearby army units, and an army field hospital just outside the town.

It was a blessing that the army hospital was there for I needed them the following week. It was only a minor matter, very bad toothache. If you had to have a tooth pulled out when you were in Mentakab you had a choice of three alternatives. One, you could travel the hundred odd miles to KL and chance getting ambushed, two, you could go to the local Chinese dentist. We had watched the Chinese dentists at work and they operated in a shop rather like a barber's shop and as you walked past you could see their "victims" squirming and on full show of the whole town. Their technique seemed to be very painful. Take one sharp knife and cut down each side of the bad tooth until you had removed enough flesh and skin to waggle it out with a pair of forceps.

The third alternative was the Medical Officer up at the hospital who admitted to me that he'd never pulled a tooth out in his life. With two burly sergeants holding onto my shoulders and my head resting back on the operating table normally used for gunshot victims, the MO took a grip on the tooth. Crack, "that's the first half out" he said triumphantly, and with the sweat standing out on my forehead, he took hold of the tooth again. He did it, and we returned to the sergeant's mess for a drink of beer which I gratefully paid for. Which of the three alternatives would you have chosen?

We had a very good wireless operator in the police station at Mentakab who daily took a SITREP of about 2,000 to 3,000 words. He could send morse and receive it at more than twenty words per minute and we promoted him to SC Corporal. I heard that after I left he went to the depot for PC training and later rose to a high rank in the force.

The town had one main street and two small streets. The main streets had *kedai* (shops) on each side and looked just like any town you would see on a Hollywood cowboy western film and we loved every dusty yard of it. We drank pretty heavily in the mess most nights and kept fit by working hard all day and playing badminton from 4pm to 5pm. After this we had tea and sandwiches, a shower, an evening meal downstairs and then got on with the serious business of drinking.

One of my part-time jobs was to give the local Chinese Home Guard some drill on the Padang. My Chinese was limited to one, two, three (*ee, eer, san*) and so after lining about 60 of them up in two or three rows, we took their shotguns to pieces by numbers and reassembled them by numbers 1-2-3 again. This went on for about 40 minutes, twice a week. It made the local Chinese feel that we trusted them enough to give them a shotgun each and they seemed to enjoy it. We didn't seem to bother much with lunch but developed rather a habit of walking across town to a small Chinese coffee shop for drinks of *susu-manis* (sweet milk) usually strawberry flavour, we liked it and we drank the small bottle of milk through straws. I bet the local.Chinese thought "there's some funny people about".

Temerloh, just down the road, held the local market every Saturday and the local Malays used to come in from the surrounding kampongs, the ladies in their finest *sarong* (*sarong kebaya*) and *baju* (*baju kurong*) and the men wearing their best *songkok* (hats).

The O/C Signals Pahang paid us a visit in the mess one day and amused us greatly with one of his stories. Apparently, he had been travelling along the road from Kuala Lipis to Jerantut in a land rover when he was fired on by terrorists from the side of the road. He was wearing shorts, unfortunately, and when he returned the fire with his sten gun, the hot "spent cartridges" were going down the leg of his shorts. So jumping up and down to shake the hot cartridge cases out of the leg of his shorts he carried on firing. He showed us the burn marks on the inside of his leg and was not amused when we laughed loudly about the incident. I decided to visit Kuala Lipis and pay my respects to everyone in the radio room there and also have a look around the state capital. The 120 mile journey would be done in a black Austin saloon car. It was a "police" car (a car used by the police around town when making private enquiries) but it was hoped that it would make Lipis and back. The driver and I wore civilian clothes and I had a black trilby hat pulled down over my face. It was a very obvious disguise but it gave me some comfort.

With a Lanchester 45 Automatic for which there was only eight rounds available and my 9mm Browning in my holster, we started the journey. Karak, Bentong, Tranum and then Raub, Benta and finally Lipis. I had heard about a police lieutenant at Tranum who had the reputation of killing about 40 terrorists in that area during the last six months. They said he was tall enough to swing a Bren machine gun supported by its sling from the hip and always led his squad from the front.

As I walked into Tranum police station I thought I vaguely recognised the police lieutenant on the far side of the charge room. Yes, it was "mummy" who we had all laughed at in Singapore. I made myself known and we chatted a while. He was quite pleased when I enquired about his mummy's health and he gave me a big wave as we continued our journey. Our previous assessment of his ability to handle the situation had been completely wrong. About six miles outside of Kuala Lipis we spotted three Buddhist monks dressed in bright orange walking ahead. I asked the driver to stop and we put them in the back for the remainder of the journey. This was no act of charity, I gave them a lift because I thought they would give us extra security on the journey. Lipis town did not impress me and I spent a dull night watching an Indian film (without sub-titles) in the local cinema, and so back to Mentakab. The friendship that existed in the lieutenants' mess in Mentakab gave us a feeling of safety and the men that were the members couldn't be bettered.

Living was easy and the food was good.

One of the lieutenants was a Scot called "Jock" of course, a very tall and solid man with a heart of gold. Unfortunately, "Jock" had a drinking problem. Brandy was his drink and he would go through a full bottle on most days.

Early in the morning he would call for the Chinese "boy" to bring him a cup of tea which was dutifully placed on the small table at the side of his bed. He would pick up the cup and pour most of the tea into a slop basin at the side of the bed, then he would pick up his brandy bottle and fill the tea cup up with brandy. Raising himself up on one elbow, with his eyes a-twinkle he would loudly announce to the world that "there's one thing I like in the morning and that's a cup of tea". Despite this bad drinking habit, he was a very likeable man, who would very rarely lose his temper and his sociable chatter was appreciated by all. Anyhow, you just had to listen to him, he was too big and powerful to ignore.

We had a radio receiver in the police signals room at the police station at Mentakab which "listened in" 24 hours a day on a fixed frequency for any emergency calls from rubber estates that were especially vulnerable to bandit attack. One of these estates was called Sungei Tekal which could be reached by rail as it was only a few stops up the line to "Tekal Halt".

I was very happy when the manager of Sungei Tekal invited me up to his estate. I accepted, of course, took the train to Tekal Halt and was then taken by the Scottish manager to his bungalow (wherever do all these Scots come from, you find them everywhere). After a magnificent breakfast, we walked around his estate. It was a palm oil estate, and the workers were mostly Tamil Indians. They worked hard cutting the fruit and nuts down from the palm trees and transporting them to the factory. Once there, the oil would be squeezed out of the fruit and nuts and be sold to their customers.

Apart from a general feeling of happiness amongst the workers, the other thing that struck me was their appearance. They were black, of course they were, they were Tamils weren't they! But they gleamed like black diamonds and it was not until I went into the factory that I realised why they literally shone in the sunlight. Because they worked amongst the palm oil, a lot of the oil was transferred to their skin and this made them look extremely healthy.

It must have been a lonely life for the manager and his assistant at Sugei Tekal, but they looked very well on it.

I was posted to Selangor, so it was goodbye to Mentakab but I will never forget those happy days.

Above pictures: Mentakab town (main street).

8. Selangor

The transfer was to the Kajang district of Selangor which, at the time, was dominated by the bandit, Liew Kon Kim. He was the leader of the terrorists' No. 1 Platoon which comprised about 40 men and 15 girls, all Chinese. He had been educated at Kajang High School and spoke very good English. Because he carried a full beard he was known locally as the Kajang Terror, or the bearded terror. His gang killed many hundreds of the local people during his reign of about four years and he was feared by everyone in the villages and kampongs in his area. In addition to this he claimed many dozens of troops and police as his victims. He was ruthless and very effective. He operated around Kajang, Sungei Besi, Serdang, Banting and the Kuala Langat Forest Reserve South.

I joined another police lieutenant at Puchong, which is only about 12 miles from Kuala Lumpur. My responsibilities included the security of Puchong Tin Mine and Killinghall Tin Mine. One morning at about six o'clock we received a telephone call from Killinghall saying that two of their tin miners and six of my Special Constables had been ambushed at about five thirty that morning.

They were travelling from their office compound to the tin dredge. They were sat in an armoured open top truck measuring some five feet by four feet and about four feet deep. The top was open and the two miners carried sterling machine guns and the SCs had rifles. It was a miniature train, pulled by a diesel motorised vehicle. The driver of the engine was a Sikh. The distance from the office area to the tin dredge was about two miles and the rail track was narrow gauge. About a half mile from the start of the journey the track turned into a right-hand bend and the bandits pulled the pins out of the grenades with string which they had attached to them. The grenades which were underneath the line exploded and simultaneously the bandits opened fire from the side of the track. Their opening burst killed the driver, but either by luck or thoughtfulness, as he slumped forward dead across the throttle, his hand remained on the throttle and the train continued on its journey. With the driver dead the bandits probably thought that the train would stop and that all they had to do was to continue firing at the tin miners and police from their ambush positions. The train proceeded at about five miles an hour and after a few minutes the bandits came out of their ambush positions and followed it up the line. The two Scottish (yes, Scottish) tin miners fired at them with their sterling machine guns and the Special Constables with their rifles. Two of the Special Constables were killed but the train continued the remainder of the journey to the tin dredge where they found relative safety. We arrived there about 20 minutes later and followed Liew Kon Kim's tracks to the edge of the swamp. Yes, it had been the bearded terror, but unfortunately we lost his tracks in the swamps.

Police Lieutenant Kirkland and I lived in a small bungalow built on stilts about 300 yards from Puchong Police Station. I took advice from him because he had been operating around Puchong for about a year. We did several patrols together in jungle and swamps to the south, and our adversary was, of course, Liew Kon Kim and his gang. The RAF Regiment Malaya had a squad there at the time and they slept under the bungalow whilst their sergeant and officer used one of our rooms above. Kirkland was well organised and had a regular stream of information coming in to him from various sources.

About 5am one morning there was a knock at the door which Kirkland answered. The caller told him that he had seen three bandits in Field 13 of Bukit Hitam (Black Hill) Estate about half an hour earlier. He told us that they were trying to collect subscription money from the tappers, they had a system which was "pay up or else". Kirkland said that he would get his jungle squad from Puchong Police Station and approach the hill from the other side. "See you up there later" he said and darted away. I went with the RAF Regiment Malaya squad and their officer, Ken. We got two trucks and took the long way around keeping well out of sight of the hill. I suppose it was about 7.30 when we stopped and de-bussed. The hill was about three miles away but the going was easy and we stopped near the hill about an hour later. The hill was planted with rubber trees and the paths where the tappers worked were traced in circles around the hill. The squad were a bit noisy and we walked round the hill looking for the reported bandits. Ken decided to rest his squad, who flopped down and started smoking and talking, fortunately not too loudly.

Ken and I began to discuss the merits of continuing the search, and as we had already gone around four or five times and the time was about 11.30 I was suggesting that we go back. Ken said, "I think we'll go around just once again".

We were both stood up almost facing each other, I was looking towards where his squad were sitting and he was looking outwards, in the opposite direction. "Berhenti" shouts Ken, which is Malay for "halt". "Berhenti" he shouts for the second time and almost immediately opened fire with his Sten gun. I spun around and saw one bandit only about ten yards away. There was only time to raise my carbine to waist height and fire about six or seven rounds directly at him. Then he disappeared behind a bush.

Ken and I walked forward to the bush but there was no sign of the bandits. Ken told me that he had seen two, but the chase was on. The squad opened up with everything they had (including the kitchen sink) and I felt a bit uncomfortable with Bren gun bursts whistling past my left ear. They ran on and I carried on walking and looking. We proceeded in the general direction along the contour where we thought that the bandits would go and eventually stopped about 150 yards down the path. They stopped and Ken said to me, "You take a Bren gun and a few men and have a look around where we first saw them"; I did this and there on the ground near the bush were many blood spots on the fallen leaves of the rubber trees.

I followed the trail back towards where the squad were stopped. When we were about half way back there was an unmistakable burst of Sten gun fire and we hurried the remainder of the distance. There we saw that they had shot a bandit dead. Apparently what had happened was that they had stopped almost exactly on the spot where the bandit was hiding. He was planning to throw a grenade amongst them when he was seen by a corporal who quickly filled him with a complete magazine of Sten from close range.

We cut a sapling, tied his wrists and his ankles, put the sapling in between and carried him down to the road. From there we telephoned Sungei Besi to report our success. He was a well-known member of the local Min Yuen and was armed with a pistol and two hand grenades. We had been lucky, the poor bandit had been unlucky. That's what it's all about, luck.

I had only been at Puchong for about three months when they gave me a proper job.

I was posted to Klang as "Staff Officer Operations Coast Circle". The OSPC (Officer Supervising Police Circle) was one of the nicest people you could ever hope to meet and he had a lovely wife with him and two gorgeous children, a boy about five years old and a girl about seven. He had been a bomber pilot during the recent war and he had some burn scars on his face which told a story. "You'll have to do until we find somebody better" he said. That cut me down to size, but as I have just said, he was a joy to work with and he always had a smile on his face.

Klang Police Station's jungle squad (mainly Chinese) were

always taken out by the same police lieutenant. When the power line which brought electricity to the town was cut and a six figure map reference given it looked like a job for the squad.

Unfortunately, the lieutenant was sick so I got "stuck" with the job of taking them out to investigate the incident.

Their usual Lt. was very good at his job, they had great confidence in him and furthermore he carried a Thompson sub-machine gun which you may know is a point four five calibre sub-machine gun which will be very effective if you point it in the right direction.

A platoon of the Suffolk Regiment was ordered to investigate the incident also, but to approach it through Midlands Estate from the southeast and I was told to approach from the southwest through North Hummock Estate. We were to meet where the power line had been cut and report back on the damage so that a repair gang could be guided back to the area. I had a lot of trouble with that squad and they were very reluctant to move as we approached the power line.

The track under the line was about ten feet wide with very thick jungle on either side. The pylons were mounted on the tops of small hills (about 70 feet high) and the wires were hanging in between them. It was a very obvious good ambush spot and when we reached the first pylon I carried on walking but the squad refused to move. I shouted at them in my most bawdy Chinese but still they refused to move. I eventually lost my temper and grabbed a Bren gun off the nearest man and walked on alone in sheer bravado. It was about 200 yards to the top of the next hill but it didn't seem to worry me (strange) and when I got to the top I looked back and signalled the squad to join me. I must have shamed them into moving for they joined me quite quickly. I continued doing this three or four times until I reached the spot where I thought the reported cut was. There was no sign of damage to the power line. There was no sign of the Suffolks and we trudged home after I told them a few home truths, in Malay this time.

When I got back into the Ops. room there was another signal from KL which said they had given us the wrong map reference previously and that the line was probably cut about four miles further out at the next bend.

The proper squad leader had now recovered from his illness and so he went the following afternoon. About four days had elapsed since the original report. I saw this police lieutenant the following day and he said, "It's a good job that you were given a wrong map reference for the two and three man prepared ambush positions I found indicated that the whole of 9 Platoon were waiting for you" and we knew from our records that they were about 40 strong and had two Brens. What was I saying about luck?

The security forces had been trying to kill Liew Kon Kim for about four years. He was one of the leading bandit leaders in the country and there was a reward of 25,000 dollars on his head. We have said that he was cunning and ruthless and that the local population lived in constant fear of him and his gang, but he was more than this, he was a living legend and a constant thorn in the side of the security forces. The police and the army had a healthy respect for Liew. His favourite areas were probably around Kajang and Banting and the jungle swamps in between these two towns.

We have said that his whole gang probably numbered more than 50 including at least ten young girls. They moved around the area quite a lot and popped up in the most unexpected places. He usually moved with about 15 to 20 bandits and the others were probably collecting food and money from the local population or sick with jungle sores and stomach troubles.

His gang, known as No. 1 Platoon, were fully uniformed and well armed. Their information about the movements of security forces was good for they had many thousands of Min Yuen and other informers working for them. We had great difficulty in obtaining any reliable information about where he was. The situation changed on that fateful morning. The Special Branch/CID set up in Klang was excellent and they were led by a brilliant Scotsman, Assistant Superintendent, a police lieutenant who looked very oriental in appearance (he did all the leg work), assisted by two or three good inspectors, sergeants, etc. The information came in early that morning from a worker on a rubber estate near the coast in the Kuala Langat area.

The Suffolks moved in platoon strength from Klang to the estate. They had been given precise information that a small number of uniformed CTs had been seen on the northeast corner of the estate about 8am that morning. The platoon was led by Lieutenant Hands. They took a small jungle track out of the northeast corner into the jungle. They had only travelled about 50 yards when they heard the sound of music playing from a small hut in a clearing about 30 yards ahead. It was the tune they always played on request programmes on Radio Malaya, which made the time precisely 11am. The platoon took cover and then moved slowly to within 15 yards of the hut. The music continued and it probably had a soothing effect on the "national service conscripts". First one person came out of the hut and had a look around and then went back, then a second bandit did the same thing. The Suffolks closed in, three bandits came out of the hut, one had a beard and one of the others was a woman, all uniformed and armed. The platoon opened fire. The bandits ran for some cover into the nearby swamps. There were four in all and Lieutenant Hands chased the one that looked like Liew further into the swamp and caught up with him. He had put on quite a bit of weight and got stuck in the swamp. A well-placed carbine round fired by one of the soldiers got Liew through the eye, and he died instantly. Two others were also killed, including the woman. The casualties included No. 1 Platoon Commander (Liew Kon Kim) and the second in command of neighbouring No. 3 Platoon. They had been having a top level meeting in the hut when they had been caught by surprise. It had been an extremely successful action by the soldiers. Well done, the Suffolk Regiment. The body was brought into Klang and after a few hours his body was tied to a spare wooden door and trailed behind a police van. The police van toured around all the towns and kampongs in the areas that Liew Kon Kim had previously terrorised. The idea of this was to show the local people that he really was dead, but the people were still afraid of him even though he was dead.

Later on, he was taken up to the mortuary at Klang Hospital and I got the job of taking two SEPs (surrendered enemy personnel) to officially recognise the body. It was not a pleasant job.

At about 10am one morning the OSPC (Officer Supervising Police Circle) said to me, "I am going out regrouping in Kuala Selangor", and off he went. This was the job of bringing the Chinese in from living in huts on the jungle edge where they were easy meat for the bandits and housing them all together in the "New Villages". The Special Constables guarded the New Villages 24 hours a day, but they didn't grumble, it was all in a day's work for these unsung heroes. The conditions in which they lived, as I have said, and the chances they continually took were unending and after all this they probably finished up being shouted at by some overpaid planter or some ignorant police officer.

The news came through that a police convoy had been ambushed in the Kuala Selangor area. Two officers dead, two wounded, three policemen killed and several other police wounded. The OSPC was one of the officers killed. No. 9 Platoon of the bandit army had put a log across the road and with the help of their two Bren guns they had cut the convoy to pieces. They even came down onto the road after the ambush and took arms and uniform from the bodies.

We went to the OSPC's funeral at the police/military section on the Ampang Road and every time I go to KL I pay the grave a visit if I have the time. He was a man worth remembering.

They pushed me out to do some real work i/c No.12 District, two jungle squads to keep busy, three police stations and about 500 assorted SCs to take care of. It was also the area where No.9 Platoon operated, charming!

Part of my system for sorting out the best SCs for the jungle squads was to go to the estates or the police stations and say to the SCs, "Mahu masuk Jungle Squad?" which means in English "Do you want to join the Jungle Squad?" I then used to ask them, "Ada cukup berani?" which means "Are you brave enough?", and finally, "Ada cukup kuat?" which means "Are you strong enough?". I then offered my hand and asked them to squeeze it as hard as they could. This scheme worked and soon we were recruiting well.

Sgt. Ismail, my SC Sergeant, an intelligent and keen man, used to find it all highly amusing and he was even more amused at Batu Tiga Police Station one morning. We were asking if there was anyone else who wanted to join and they said that there was just one more and that we would find him behind the police station. We went around and noticed some dumb-bells and other strength developing equipment laying around but took no particular notice of it. He was small, even for a Malay, and had curly hair and laughing eyes. I offered my hand and asked him to squeeze it as hard as he could. It was an extremely painful experience for he had a grip like a vice and he held on until I shouted for him to stop. We had found a good man and he soon made Corporal. The north end of my division, which included Petaling Jaya and Pilmoor Estate are now occupied by KL International Airport and a modern housing estate, times change don't they?

I picked up a Chinese SC at Petaling Jaya Police Station, which was unusual, you didn't find many Chinese in the police and we put him with his kit into the back of the land rover. The vehicle was left in the office compound of Glenmarie Estate at the 12th mile and I got out and went for a cold drink up to my little bungalow about 100 yards up the hill on the estate. I heard two or three shots coming from amongst the rubber trees near the office compound. The estate manager was screaming "stop him shooting". The Chinese SC wandered into the office compound and I went up to him and asked him for his rifle. He surrendered it without any trouble.

He told us that he had been shooting at a lot of bandits which he had seen up in the air. We put him in the land rover and took him to Klang Hospital who could offer us no help. He went back to Petaling Jaya. It seemed to us that it was clearly a question of "cold feet", and he was just acting crazy to avoid being taken to Rasak. We had a jungle squad at Rasak.

Klang and Rasak

Klang was the town where we relaxed when we were off duty. The rest house, the Klang Club and the Coast Club were our usual meeting places. In fact I lived at the rest house in one of their rooms for several months during that time. The food which was prepared by the two Chinese owners was very good and we had no complaints about the service they provided.

The town was a reasonably safe place but one night there was an incident which made us realise that the enemy were around. The police lieutenant from Special Branch in Klang had been with us for the evening and we had all enjoyed his company immensely. Most of the "crowd" had either left the rest house or gone to their rooms. He was one of the last to leave and so it was very quiet as he made his way towards the front door. As he got near the front door he heard the distinct clicks of the hammers of two pistols being cocked.

With a quick movement he threw himself down flat on the floor and quickly fired two shots from his Browning pistol. Two shots came back in return from the Min Yuen who had been waiting for him. The bandits then quickly scurried away back to wherever they had come from. It had been a close shave for him but the incident did not seem to arouse a lot of interest, in fact life went on as if nothing unusual had happened at all.

A few evenings later a friend of mine who ran Bukit Kemuning Police Station was with us. He was a good looking man of about twenty five years old and his contribution to the evening's entertainment was usually the singing of one or two popular songs. He had a good tenor voice and his songs were usually nostalgic about his "loved one far across the sea" or some similar "tear jerking" words which usually had us eating out of his hand. There's nothing like a well-sung sentimental song to quieten down a party and bring them all back to their senses before they went home.

"Would you like to come back to Kemuning with me?" he asked. It was about eleven o'clock and he had a land rover and a driver so I gratefully accepted his offer. All went well as we travelled the first half mile of the two mile journey. It had been a good evening and the straight drive back along a safe road put us in a relaxed state of mind.

We were taken by surprise when several shots rang out from the rubber trees on our left hand side. The driver was told to put his foot down and we both emptied a magazine of our Brownings into the trees on the side of the road. We couldn't see anybody but I became more concerned with the speed of the vehicle which was now doing more than seventy miles an hour. I shouted to the driver to slow down, which he did and we reached Kemuning a few minutes later. We telephoned Klang Police Station and reported the incident.

There was a detention centre (for suspect terrorists) about five hundred yards from that road and they had also reported an incident which had happened about the same time as ours. It seems that they had seen figures in the rubber trees near to their perimeter wire and had opened fire. They said that the fire had been returned. The following day we began to wonder if there had indeed been any bandits at all on the previous evening or was it just a case of the camp guards and us shooting at each other.

The Rasak Jungle Squad had to be trained and few jungle edge jaunts seemed to be indicated. Now, monkeys of all shapes and sizes can cause one a lot of trouble for at about one hundred yards, two or three of them standing on their back legs can look just like people and on several occasions they caused us to get into a real panic. One day it was even worse, we were investigating reports that a small group of bandits had been seen in a patch of jungle just north of Midlands Estate and so we followed up the information. We had gone into the jungle about two hundred yards and were travelling very quietly in single file because the bush was very thick. A loud crashing sound straight ahead had Sgt. Ismail and I throwing ourselves behind a fallen tree and the crashing sound came closer and closer. As we waited for the bandits to appear, our hearts were not too happy for we were pretty thin up front. They did appear, but they weren't bandits of course, they were several large monkeys and it was them that had us shaking in our boots. They scooted off when they saw us. Monkeys, you can keep them.

The Malay SCs amused us from time to time and on this particular occasion when we were on a morning patrol one of them refused to go on any further.

"What's the matter?" I said, "Ada takut?" (which means "Are you afraid?"). "No Sir" he replied, "Saya belum kawin lagi". I didn't know the phrase and when the sergeant had stopped laughing I asked him what the SC had said. He says he is not married yet and that is why he doesn't want to go. As they say, "there was no answer to that". I asked the sergeant to deal with it and after a few choice words which probably included a few veiled threats which were promises of fates worse than death, the patrol continued and the SC looked a lot happier. Ismail was a nice man but he could be tough when the need arose.

We took a path along the jungle fringe and we were again travelling in single file (five yards apart, of course) when suddenly there was an ear-piercing scream from behind. I turned to see the fourth or fifth SC in the file jumping about three feet in the air and shouting loudly at the same time. Again the sergeant got lumbered with finding out what was wrong. The patrol was continuing to loop around the jumping point but within a few minutes Ismail came back to report, "It's a cobra, but it looks asleep, anyway it's not moving". I decided to let sleeping cobras sleep and we continued on our way.

*   *   *   *   *   *

The Contingent Armourer arrived to check all weapons in the Division. It took him a few days and last of all he asked to look at my Sten gun.

"Not likely" I replied, "I have carried this weapon with me for more than six months nobody touches my Sten". Of course he insisted and as he had the authority, I had no alternative but to let him inspect it. Within a few minutes he had thrust the weapon back towards me with a grunt saying, "the firing pin is so worn that I doubt if it would even fire, the pin is only just level with its casing and it should protrude. I'm not giving this weapon back to you, go and get yourself another one". I picked up a carbine this time, they are lighter, carry about 12 rounds in the magazine and the spare magazines are small and can be slipped into almost any pocket.

Now the Min Yuen from the Batu Tiga and Rasak areas had been going to Sungei Way Estate at the end of every month to collect subscriptions from the workers on the estate and it was reported that they travelled along the railway line at the back of Glenmarie Estate. I decided to do a couple of night ambushes to try and catch them "with their trousers down".

We didn't get anybody, but these ambushes caused me a lot of sweat. The bushes on the bank where we lay doing the ambushes were very spikey and had a tendency to get stuck on your clothes, but that was the least of my worries. Because we had not been issued with grenade pouches, we had to look after our grenades as best we could. You could hook them on your belt, place them on the ground in front of you as you lay in ambush or hold one or two in your hands. None of these were very satisfactory when you remember that during the few hours we spent rolling about on the bank we also had to cope with the midges and mosquitoes. There was a constant fear that we might accidentally pull out the grenade ring that was attached to the grenade pin.

We only did two of these ambushes but we thought that was too many.

Soon I was to have the treat of a lifetime. I had to go up to Rasak Estate one night about nine o'clock to see the manager and so I took the two mile long road from Batu Tiga. The road was very narrow and the rubber trees and lalang on each side was quite thick. It was dipped headlights most of the way but just a few hundred yards short of the estate I decided to put my headlights on full. Almost immediately the headlights clearly picked out a black panther leaping across the road. What a sight, he was about nine or ten feet long and was fully stretched as he jumped. He looked so graceful and was jet black, how lucky I had been to see him.

I decided to teach the Rasak squad the rudiments of bayonet fighting even though we had no bayonets and they enjoyed it immensely as they rushed around sticking their imaginary bayonets into imaginary victims and of course there was the added bonus of the screaming and shouting that accompanies every bayonet charge. The Tamil labourers on the estate looked very impressed and the moral of the squad went up a few notches.

I went into Klang and asked the OCPD if he could get us any bayonets from Police HQ in KL. He said that he would ask them. A few days later we got our reply. The police is a defensive force and the bayonet is an offensive weapon and therefore they could not issue them to us. I was very disappointed and so were the squad. Apart from getting completely lost on a few occasions our expeditions went well and we didn't have any casualties and that's got to be good.

One way of not getting killed

After a bit of experience, a few jungle edge jaunts, plus some good advice from some friends, I thought I'd try a few days' proper jungle work.

Rations for three days, which for the Malays meant rice and a few assorted spices and a bit of chicken or fish or both (if you planned on having a party). Chillies, both green and red, were also a necessity. For me it was a few tins of meat and vegetable stew, some plain biscuits and, of course, a little bacon and the essential tea, sugar and milk. Tommy cookers were used to heat the food up (solid paraffin wax) and they were very good and simple to use.

It was important not to come out of the jungle the same way that you went in. Using the same routes on a regular basis or coming back from anywhere or doing anything habitually would draw the attention of the local bandits and of course they would make their plans accordingly.

You must always keep your eyes open and move leisurely, yet deliberately and, of course, quietly. No talking, just use sign language with your hands and arms. If you don't know the signals normally used, then develop your own and practise before you start sticking your neck out.

You normally patrol with platoon strength, three sections of seven plus a corporal for each section, a sergeant and you, that's twenty six. You certainly never move with less than two sections, that would be suicide, for everyone has to be covered. When you stop to rest, spread out and keep quiet, find yourself a convenient spot where you can see around you and yet still have good cover. Stop patrolling about 3.30 to 4.00pm and then choose a place to camp for the night which, if possible, should be easy to defend, say on a hill with running water nearby for bathing. On this issue, don't forget to have one section covering the other section which is having a bath.

You will find that one of your greatest enemies in the jungle are leeches. They get everywhere, and I mean **everywhere** and you can guarantee that at the end of the day everyone will have four or five leeches on them. They bury their heads into your skin and the more blood they suck the fatter they become. They start off about the size of half a matchstick and when they've had enough they can be as fat as your thumb. To get their heads out, just touch them on the tail with a lighted cigarette and they will drop off you. Do not try to pull them off for they will break in half and the head will stay in your body which, within a few days, turns into an infectious wound. You have to do this for each other, of course, for many of the leeches get on your back.

Put three or four sentries around the camp, about thirty yards out and get the rice cooking. Then make yourself comfortable for the night by building some make-do shelters made of bamboo and attap and cover it with your ground sheet to keep out the rain.

There are two important times in camp, morning stand-to and evening stand-to. Each man takes up a position around the camp making sure that he picks a good position and that he knows it well.

You stand-to from half an hour before darkness to half an hour after dark which is usually from about quarter past six to quarter past seven. In the event of an alarm each man will go to his stand-to position and wait for orders. Stand-to in the morning is usually from six o'clock to seven o'clock. Trip wires with grenades attached must be put out at all approaches to the camp and the wire should be about three feet high so that animals could get under without setting off the grenade. I sometimes put a piece of string to my legs and ran it out to the weakest part of our defence each night. I did get an occasional "pull" but always a false alarm.

The jungle is quiet during the day and quite noisy at night. The animals will not attack you unless you disturb them, so stear clear of them and you won't be bothered. The snake King Cobra is the exception, he will attack on sight and his bite is deadly. His sight is not good but he moves very fast, so step quickly to one side and either hit him or take a shot at him as he hopefully goes past you.

Getting ready to go out on patrol.

Posing for the camera after the patrol ended.

Bringing a patrol out of the
jungle swamp.

Exhausted in the jungle.

Resting amongst the rubber trees.

9. Enjoying Ourselves

One of the most pleasant times that I had whilst in the Klang area was to go "wild pig shooting" on Kering Island. The manager of Sungei Rasak Estate had a small boat moored at Port Swettenham and he occasionally took it across to Kering Island. It only took about half an hour of "chugging" through the channels between the islands off Swettenham to reach the island. I don't know where the six or seven Tamil Indians came from, but they were waiting for us on the island when we got there and they had about ten or 12 fierce looking dogs. The dogs had scars received from previous encounters with the wild boars, whose tusks can inflict a severe wound, and the scars were on the noses and faces of the dogs.

We all had double-barrel shotguns but the best shot was a Chinese man we called "Gregg" and he had an automatic shotgun.

The Tamils knew where the pigs were and Gregg positioned us where the pig tracks entered the clearings. They then took the dogs around the other side of the small clump of jungle. When we heard the dogs barking we knew they had disturbed a pig and that it was running along one of the tracks; would they appear at the end of our track, we wondered? After a few false alarms, one eventually did bolt out from the bush and we had a quick pot-shot at him or her, but we didn't hit anything. We all assembled at the end of the operation and found that the party had bagged two wild pigs. We wondered who we had to congratulate. Of course, it was Gregg who had got them both. We felt quite ashamed, and we were supposed to be the professionals. We found out later that his plan was to wait about thirty yards behind us and pick them off at his leisure, but seriously, he was a very good shot. At the end of it all one of the Tamils would climb a coconut tree and drop a few coconuts down to us on the ground. The cool milk from the inside of the coconut was very refreshing. It was a simple pleasure, but we enjoyed it immensely.

The best part of our picnic was yet to come, for the Sungei Rasak Manager was no fool. He used to bring his Chinese cook with him and on the way back the boat would be anchored off a sandy beach, we swam in the cool water and on getting back into the boat we would find a delightful curry and rice waiting for us.

Another enjoyable job fell to me one night when I was duty officer in Klang. One of my stops was the Chinese Club in the centre of the town and of course they were all playing cards as usual, but this time I caught them out with a lot of money on the tables. It was illegal and I pointed this out to the owner and he was speechless. There must have been at least seventy or eighty Chinese in the Club when I decided that this was my big moment. The owner knew that he could lose his licence and the players knew they could be pro-secuted, I had a captive audience. I spoke to the assembled sorry-looking bunch of Chinese men for about half an hour on the evils of Communism and why it was their duty to help us rid Malaya of these evil pests. They listened, they had to, and I left with a smile and a wave when I thought the message had been received. Doubtless many Min Yuen in the Club would report the talk back to the local CTs.

What shall we do tonight? The station sergeant suggested that a few of us should pay the local 'drug scene' a visit and try and pick up a few specimens. One of the places they used was a large wooden building partitioned off into rooms mea-suring about fifteen feet square. There were corridors run-ning through the building, but you could get to some of the rooms from outside. The system was to choose a door and get through it quickly. We did this and found three Chinese men passing an opium pipe from one to the other. The opium lamp was burning in the middle and doing its job of warming up the opium pellets as they were prepared for the customers by the den's owner. We pulled them out of the room and bundled them into the police van, they had sick grins on their faces, they didn't know where they were or where they were going. In fact, by the looks on their faces, you would have thought that they were off for a weekend at Port Dickson or Penang. We collected the pipes and the opium pellets, which smelt a bit like licorice and dropped them off at the police station. The sergeant was pleased and locked them up gleefully. What a different sight the following morning. The men looked completely shattered, they were obviously ill and all of them were very thin. Drug smokers spend every cent they have on the drugs and neglect themselves and their wives and children. A few weeks later in Court the magistrate asked me which of the men I had actually seen smoking the opium. I replied that as I entered the room they were passing the pipe from one to the other. "Then you didn't actually see anyone smoking?" he said, I had to reply "no" and they were let go free on a technicality.

Food

KL was a wonderful place in those days. Delicate aromas hung around every street from where Batu Road joined Victory Avenue past the main Padang and as far up as where it joined the Pahang Road just past Campbell Road. If you wanted a straight-forward English kind of meal, it was easy. I have mentioned the good ones, the Coliseum, Nanto's "Milk" Bar, the KK Hotel and the like and the Selangor Club, though pricey, was reputed to be good. We knew they wouldn't let us in so we never found out.

I decided that I would be adventurous and follow that aroma, so off I went to sample the local food. Strangely enough, good curry meals were hard to find in KL in those days and even these days you'll be very lucky to find one. There was one, and only one, on Batu Road just opposite the Coliseum. The outside was painted green and that's how you recognised it. It was an Indian restaurant and you went upstairs to eat. The curry gravy was served separately in a large, hot dish and placed in the middle of the table.

Then the waiters would ceremoniously serve curried fish, curried chicken, curried lamb and other curried dishes each on their own plate and each containing enough of each kind of food to satisfy the appetite of three or four people. Finally, a very large dish filled with boiled rice would be put on the table. The various curried dishes were cooked to perfection and were very hot (that is, curry hot). First, you put enough rice on the plate to satisfy your expected needs and then chose curried chicken, fish, lamb or whatever you felt like eating. Top it off with the hot curry sauce and start eating. If you felt like second helpings, they were there on the table and you could help yourself again. It was a feast fit for a king, or maybe I should have said, a sultan.

But now to the serious stuff. The half-hour downpour which seemed to occur on most late afternoons always seemed to be a prelude of better things to come. The streets looked cleaner, the dust had gone and the appetite began to rise as if tasting the unexpected.

The evening traffic trundled along the main street as the trishaw and rickshaw men struggled manfully with their loads. Most people were going home after a day's work and did not seem to notice the changing scene on the pavements. Most of the goods which had been on display in the shop windows and on the pavements of the footpath had vanished. It was now about six o'clock in the evening, the stragglers were still making their weary way homewards, but a different stage was being set up on Batu Road. As if by magic, hundreds of food stalls appeared. They arrived by trishaw, rickshaw, or were simply just mobile cafés which were just pulled into position by their owners. Within half an hour of darkness falling another KL started to live. Soon the sweet smell of cooking food hung heavily in the air. Some stalls cooked their food on slow-burning charcoal-fed stoves. Others were more adventurous and needed fierce hot flames to heat up their large frying pans (woks). A few stools were littered around for customers, but most just sat on the pavement or on a low wall or in Chinese style, just sat on their haunches. We usually took the food with us and sat in the car to enjoy it. The favourites were Mah-mee, Mee hoon, Nasi Goreng. Mah-mee and mee hoon are usually long noodles which have been boiled, after adding bean shoots and any other vegetables that were popular. The final flavour is decided by the amount of soy sauce that the cook added to it. Nasi goreng is fried rice. First, you soak the rice in cold water for about half an hour and then you gently boil it for about 20 minutes or so. The final boiling should get rid of all of the excess water and should be done slowly. The boiled rice is then taken and fried in oil over a hot stove and fried quite quickly. Again, add soy sauce as you go along, but not too much. Maybe you fancy Yu Chi (Shark's Fin). It is usually reserved for special occasions and can be very expensive. It does, of course, contain finely chopped Shark's Fin, and it is stir fried with chopped onions, ginger, mushrooms, chicken stock, breast of chicken, peeled prawns and, of course, a little soy sauce. The soup has a thick consistency and simply slides down your throat. It can be a very good appetizer for your meal.

You may choose Zha Jiang Mian (noodles in meat sauce), or maybe you fancy Chow Mein which are fried noodles. Egg foo yong is good and is fried rice with added whisked-up egg. Chinese sweet and sour pork are favourites with the Chinese, the sweetness being obtained by adding pineapple to the dish. My favourite was deep fried King prawns with fried rice. The prawns have to be cleaned and washed, dried and then coated with a batter which when it is placed in very hot fat for five or six seconds, turns into a very crispy coating for the prawns. You could, of course, buy these dishes in most ordinary Chinese restaurants, but they did not seem to have the taste or the atmosphere of our friendly kerbside cafés.

Satay is popular with everyone and are small pieces of meat, fried in oil over a hot stove after first being dipped into a sauce made from the cook's secret recipe. They are then stuck onto a thin, wooden stick and carried away to be eaten at the leisure of the customers as they walk along chatting their merry way to dreamland.

The British soldiers swayed from bar to bar, never interfering with these happy people and when they'd had enough stumbled clumsily back to barracks, and to bed. The soldiers had a dangerous job to do and the locals seemed to understand that they needed these periods of relaxation.

10. John Chapman

The school certificate was normally taken at the end of the fourth year in the grammar school which John Chapman attended. Unfortunately, at the end of his third year, the school authorities decided that pupils in the lowest two third year forms would have to stay on an extra year which meant that he would take the certificate at the end of the fifth year. The prospect of another two years at school unnerved him and so he asked his father if he could leave school and start work. He came from a very poor working class family but because John seemed sure that he wanted to leave, they reluctantly agreed.

He was good at Chemistry and Physics and was soon working for ICI as an hourly paid laboratory worker. He was under 17 years old when the war started and by telling a lie about his age, he managed to join the local Infantry regiment. The training he received in discipline and weapons would prove very useful to him a few years later, but he didn't know it then. Nine months or so later the army finally realised how old he was and transferred John, along with about fifty other young soldiers, to the Coast Defence Artillery. His old Infantry battalion was sent into action and many never returned. The war never seemed to touch John, maybe he was too immature, maybe his guardian angel was looking after him, but after serving four years overseas in Africa and Italy (including a sea-borne landing at Salerno in Italy) he returned to civilian life as if he had never been a soldier. He couldn't get a decent job; he tried to gain a science qualification at evening college classes and finally found himself teaching radio theory to ex-servicemen in a private college.

Then fate took a hand. He saw the advertisement and so he applied to be a police lieutenant in Malaya. He had to look at his school atlas to find it on the map and when he eventually did, the location didn't mean very much to him. Geography had never been one of his strong subjects at school.

The date for the London interview had been arranged and he went down to it at the Crown Agents 4, Millbank, London. Immediately after the interview he had to go to Harley Street for a strict medical examination. "Harley Street" said the London taxi-driver, "Blimey, mate, it will cost you a guinea to ring the bell there". After his medical examination, he returned to the Crown Agents. They told him that they would write and let him know if he had been successful with his application. He then spent a week with the territorial army, training. On arriving back home he found a letter from his employer giving him notice of termination of employment and enclosing his national insurance cards. Apparently, the Crown Agents had written to them for a reference, which they presumably sent and then sent a letter to him giving him the "sack". He telephoned the Crown Agents in London. He asked them if he had got the appointment or not. The letter was in the post, they said, and John had to wonder for another day about his employment position. It arrived the following morning and it said that the Crown Agents were pleased to advise him, etc., and would he make arrangements to take the plane from London to Singapore at 9am on the 15th of September, 1950.

"Would passengers for Qantas flight 179 please board the aircraft". It was 9am and they took their seats. The engines started, stopped, started again and then stopped again. This was repeated several times and then there came another announcement, "Would passengers please leave the aircraft, we have a slight technical problem, but hope to be taking off soon". He did take off later, but it was one o'clock in the afternoon when the four engined turbo-prop. finally left the ground. The flight was for Rome, Cairo, Bahraine, Karachi and finally Singapore. The pilot announced that they would not now be landing in Rome but that they had taken on extra fuel and would be flying straight through to Cairo.

The Constellation aircraft was high over the alps and it was dark outside. One bright passenger passed the word around that the outside engine on the right hand side hadn't got a red flame coming out of it any more and that the bright light from the inner right side engine was spluttering fire one moment, then stopping and spitting fire once again. Five to ten minutes elapsed and the pilot made this announcement, "We've developed a fuel leak on the starboard side. I'm heading out to sea to jettison our extra fuel into the sea but we expect to arrive in Rome in about 30 minutes' time". "Rome," said John to his seat companion, "I thought we were going straight through to Cairo". The "fasten your seat belts" sign came on, and almost immediately the aeroplane banked sharply, and went into a steep nose-dive. They seemed to be losing height very quickly. Was this the end, thought John. He hadn't even started yet. Didn't the pilot know that he'd got a job to do in Malaya? About an hour later they made a forced landing at Rome Airport. They stayed in a hotel in Rome for two days whilst the aircraft was being repaired. John was not very happy with flying after that and was grateful to land in Singapore in one piece. He had to go through the kitting-out procedure at HMS Terror like we had done and probably had the same misgivings about what the future held for him.

John took the night train from Singapore to Kuala Lumpur and before he left, inquisitively examined the two crash wagons which the train was to push along as it journeyed north. They were quite long and rectangular in shape and the idea was, as we have said before, that if the bandits tampered with the railway track the crash wagons would come off the line and the driver would hopefully have time to pull the train to a halt. The train was "fired on" just south of Labis near a place called Jagoh. The new police lieutenant slept through it all. One civilian who was killed was a fifty three year old Indian gentleman and the other person killed was a young Chinese lady about thirty years old. John listened in disbelief when he was told the story.

Police Lieutenant Chapman was invited to a Chinese dinner at a hotel on Bukit Bintang Road by the manager of the hotel. He had no idea why he got the invitation, but he went. It was a grand affair and there were between fifty and one hundred persons present. It would be about thirty courses, so they had told him. It started with the traditional Shark's Fin and then, one by one, the large plates containing each course were placed in the centre of the tables. You just helped yourself from the centre plate and took what you wanted. If you liked the dish, you had one or two pieces or even more, but if you didn't, you only had one piece or maybe none at all. The meal lasted for about two hours and the brandy and ginger ale kept in a regular appearance. The host kept on announcing the dish that they were being served, this is boneless chicken he would say, this is boneless mutton, this is boneless fish, this is boneless lamb and so it continued until the end of the meal. When the meal was over, John felt sure that he had a small bone stuck in his throat. He tried to ignore it but throughout the night sleep was difficult because of the constant pain when he tried to swallow his own saliva. The next morning a visit to the local hospital was a must and within half an hour they had him on the operating table. It did not take long and after it was all over they showed him a very thin, sharp bone which they had taken out of his throat. He was put inside an ambulance for the return journey and in it he found that he had a companion. He was a contract Assistant Superintendent of Police who said he worked at police headquarters and that his name was Peers. "You've heard of Donald Peers, the singer" he said, "Well, I'm his brother". He had certainly had heard of the singer, Donald Peers, who hadn't? He was currently top of the British hit parade, with his song "By a Shady Nook". He was certainly pleased to have met his brother and it was a story he told several times to his friends.

The party was over and John was posted to Kamayan Police Station near Triang. Now Triang was a very bad area, thick with bandits and not the sort of place you would pick for a tea party. But the party was not quite over. One of the local kampongs was throwing a Ronggeng dance and there would be Joget dancing also, and so he gladly accepted the invitation. There were plenty of girls there, mostly Malay and he noticed that one of the men dancers stood out from the rest. You couldn't help but notice him. He was taller than the average Malay man, good-looking and had black, wavy hair. The most noticeable thing about him was his carefree manner and his happy smile, which seemed to develop into a handsome grin every so often.

Quite a few Malay princes were there, so they were saying, and soon the slow rhythmic music of the ronggeng started. It was enchanting to watch this dance for the first time. The dancers glided towards each other in rhythm with the music, as they approached one another they appeared to hesitate and then passed each other only to turn a few steps later and come back again in a swaying, entrancing movement. This time, they would approach and then stop and turn away from one another. It was just like life's meetings between men and women, he thought. The joget was faster and was enjoyed by all. He made enquiries about the tall man, and they told him that his name was Yeop Mahidin who was personal assistant to the Sultan of the State and the leader of the kampong guards. He had a reputation of being a fearless fighter and had been successful on many occasions against the local bandits. He had been brought up in the area and knew many of the bandits personally. He certainly knew

Abdullah C.D. the local terrorist leader, for he was Yeop Mahidin's cousin.

Kuala Krau, just up the railway line from Kamayan, was attacked by about 300 bandits, they burnt down the railway station and many houses in the town. Their next target was the police station and, though they killed four policemen and four of the women inside the police compound, they failed to capture it. John and a police patrol were sent to relieve Kuala Krau. They travelled along the railway by armoured train and pulled into an embankment about 100 yards from the town.

There was a bandit lying down behind a Bren gun on top of the embankment. John took careful aim with his carbine, crack, the bandit rolled over. Another bandit took his place behind the Bren gun and John took another shot and again made a kill. This happened four times, four shots and four dead bandits. Unbelievable, but true. The patrol stayed in the armoured train and took pot-shots whenever they could. John said afterwards that he didn't think the bandits knew exactly where they were on the train, which was just as well when you consider their numbers and the size of John's squad (about fifteen).

About half an hour later a bugle sounded and the bandits left the town. They had occupied the town for about two days. John went back to Kemayan and very soon was called out again. Two hundred bandits, led by the local folk hero, Abdullah C.D., had attacked Kemayan Estate and burnt down all the estate buildings, including the manager's bungalow. When Police Lieutenant Chapman arrived on the scene, Abdullah C.D. had gone. This incident reminds me of another P/Lt. in that area who was stationed down the river at Mengkarak. He was a very nice, well-spoken man, with good manners and an attention for detail. His one great failing was that he could not seem to be able to learn to speak the Malay language. As you can imagine, this was a great handicap to him. He tried to learn the language but with very little success. He did learn one word, however, and that was "maybe" or "barangkali", as the Malays say. So every time his Special Constables approached him with a question or a problem he would answer "maybe". Eventually, he became Tuan Maybe, Tuan Barangkali. A pity to be known as Mr Maybe, not everyone can learn foreign languages and he certainly paid for it.

John was kept very busy around Triang for the next few months and had one or two contacts with the bandits but without success.

They decided to do a screening operation of Kemayan village and so at 6am one morning the kampong guards, which when included with the Special Constables numbered over one hundred, began screening the houses. The idea was that you entered every house and searched for bandits that may be hiding there and any arms and ammunition you may find. This was the first time he had been on a screening operation, but it appeared to be simple enough. The ground was wet, for a little rain had fallen during the night, and John approached his first house. He banged at the door and then kicked when there was no reply. He heard sounds from behind the door. His heart missed a beat as he visualised a bandit crouching on the other side with shotgun ready. Safety catch off, so he thought, and his finger rested lightly on the trigger. He heard the sound of something falling on the ground in front of his feet and realised that he had pushed the magazine release catch by mistake. Whilst he was searching for the magazine on the floor, for it was still quite dark, the door swung open. He did not find his magazine immediately, but what he did find when he looked up was an old Chinese lady who proceeded to tell him off in Chinese, and in no uncertain terms. Though he could speak no Chinese at all he seemed to get the drift of her loud comments, "What are you doing banging so loudly at my door so early in the morning?" He found his magazine, smiled at the lady and didn't go into the house. Luck had been with him and he didn't think that he would tempt it any more that morning.

Apart from John's careless mistake, the operation was a success. The SCs and kampong guards had surprised two sleeping terrorists (one was shot and killed) and the other was captured. They also arrested about ten suspected bandit sympathisers.

When he had been at Kemayan for about a year he knew that he wanted a break and what better place to spend it in than Kuala Lumpur? It would be no fun by himself so he arranged a trip down-river to Kampong Chenor and paid Paul a visit. He was just the company John needed. Paul especially had a lonely life at Chenor and was suffering from jungle sores and was generally in very poor condition. They talked and talked, especially Paul who, apart from the occasional conversation with Sukaimy, his wireless operator, seldom spoke a word of English to anybody. The date was fixed and the OCPD Temerloh, who had a car, would come down with them. The great day arrived, it was Friday morning and soon the three of them were on their way to the big city. Who cared if there were burnt-out buses on the road (relics of recent ambushes) and that the chances of being ambushed were about even? They were Europeans in a private car and they would be fair game for any terrorists.

They were just passing through a cutting after they had passed Semantan Estate when "bang" and the car swerved out of control but, luckily, stayed on the road. Ambush was their first thought. They got out hesitantly and, after a few minutes, realised that it had been a puncture. Paul took his carbine, climbed up the cutting and acted as sentry whilst the other two changed the wheel, using the spare. They continued and were near Karak when "bang" again. This time it had to be an ambush for sure they thought, but incredulously, it turned out to be another puncture. They had run out of spare wheels and decided to stop any passing cars to see if they had any wheels that might fit theirs. Not many civilian cars passed that way but after about half an hour and after stopping some eight or ten cars, they found one that fitted the bill. With a bit of gentle persuasion the Chinese driver sold them his spare and they continued the journey.

Over Genting and then it was all down-hill to KL. They stayed at the Hotel Metropole, now renamed the Hotel Malaysia and, in those days, it was one of the best hotels in the city. Soon they were sitting in the restaurant, sipping ice cold beer, gazing hungrily at the menu and contemplating the night which lay ahead. It was Nanto's, the Eastern Cabaret, more food at a wayside stall and then back to bed, was it three or was it four in the morning? They couldn't remember, but it was a very enjoyable night. They had a complete weekend's rest, if you could call it that, and returned to relate their experiences to any unsuspecting police officer or Malay who was prepared to listen. He had not been soaking up the local scenery very long when a signal came through transferring him back to KL. How lucky could you get? He was to go into the control room at High Street Police Station and take his turn over a 24 hour period with two other police lieutenants and a police inspector. They had to receive police 99 calls and direct the police patrol cars to the incident scenes. The job was monotonous, but the rewards were the freedom of Kuala Lumpur in his off-duty time. He played an April Fool's Day joke on the police lieutenant who was relieving him on the morning of the 1st. He had been on duty all the previous night and before he left to go to bed at the KK Hotel where he was staying, he left a bogus message for the P/Lt. coming on duty to report to the Superintendent i/c ops. for a special job. The hoax even reached the Chief Police Officer (CPO) and when he was ready (what was all the fuss about?) he was well and truly taken to task for his joke. What was wrong with these chair-bound people? Didn't they know that April 1st goes on even in Malaya?

The job had its lighter moments, though, for one night he answered a 99 call to be greeted with a loud shouting of "Get me out. Get me out". After some time he managed to get the address from the frightened caller, who then suddenly was cut off. The patrol car lost no time in racing to the scene and much to their surprise found a drunken European planter who had obviously been very drunk, fast asleep with the telephone still in his hand. He was in a private club and had been locked in accidentally by the club's staff when they went home, or did they just get fed up with him and left him to rot when they had difficulty persuading him to leave? We shall never know the answer, but it was funny at the time. I don't suppose the European thought it was funny to wake up at the early hours of the morning in the dark, not quite knowing where you were. But it was his own bloody fault and it was just one of those things.

John then did six months in Johor for his sins, and didn't enjoy it a bit, for Johor was probably the worst area in the country for bandit atrocities. His contract was finished, and John decided to take a few days' leave in Penang before returning to England. He had made a quick decision and was in uniform when he strolled into KL Railway Station the night he was due to take the train to Butterworth (where you get off for Penang). The office clerk in the booking office examined his leave pass and then taking something from under the counter, he handed it to John, "You're senior officer on the train tonight, Sir. Please wear this armband". On it were the words "OC Train" (Officer Commanding Train).

Was he proud? Of course he was, if they had made him Commissioner of Police or given him a knighthood he could not have felt prouder. He savoured the moment when he had to walk through the bar and heads turned. OC Train. Was there a higher position in the whole of Malaya, he wondered. If there was he'd never heard of it. He quickly came down from cloud nine and got on with the job. Visit the sentries posted between carriages, usually British soldiers and give a glance at the machine gun post at the front. Everything seemed quiet and north from Kuala Lumpur was usually a smooth ride. What could he do but retire to bed in "his" sleeping compartment and sleep like a baby till morning. He will probably always remember that night, I know that I would have.

11. The Jungle

We had finished for the day and were sitting either on the edges of our hastily erected shelters, on the ground, or just leaning against one of the many tall trees when he arrived. He had not come by invitation and, to tell you the truth, he didn't look as if he needed an invitation.

We were in a clearing on the high ground, in deep jungle in the Kulim area of Perak. It had been an eventful patrol and we were just finishing a twelve-day stint. Two airdrops had to be taken and we had done two night ambushes and, of course, the routine patrolling had to be done. But let's get back to it. He just arrived, he was a small monkey who ambled in on four legs and walked deliberately straight through our camp. In the centre of the camp was a very tall tree and, after pausing for a brief moment, he climbed up the tree very quickly. When he reached the top he looked down, just once, and then disappeared into a clump of foliage. We were obviously the intruders, he lived there, it was his tree, his house, and why should he (or she) break the habits of a lifetime? We didn't move a muscle (those of us that had any), we were fascinated, besides being quite small, he was brown and I must admit his head did seem a bit bald, giving him quite a comical appearance. We smiled at each other as he got in bed for the night. Cheeky little runt, we thought, what a nerve, but we had to admit that the tree in the middle of our camp was his tree and probably always would be.

Our bashas (jungle sleeping arrangements) were built basically by using stakes of small sapling trees driven into the ground, two of them at one end of the dwelling were about four feet tall and the two at the other end about two feet tall. They were knocked into the soft jungle ground quite easily and were spaced so that their width and length were sufficient to fit one man or sometimes two, or more. More saplings were cut and secured with rattan around the "box" about three or four inches above the ground. The floor of the bed was then interlaced with anything we could find, split bamboo if we could find any, but we usually used small saplings, ferns or anything that could take our weight and was soft. We then ceremoniously draped our ground sheets across the top, to provide cover from any rain that might penetrate the roof top green canopy on high.

After 'stand-to' in the morning we made special preparations for the airdrop that we were due to receive that day. A quick wash and some breakfast and then the parangs, axes and saws (if we had any) came out . . . four, five or even six of the large trees had to be felled, it was not an easy job. The Dropping Zone clearing was usually just outside the camp perimeter (we did not touch Charlie's tree) and after about two hours' hard work we had cleared enough jungle to take the chutes they were dropping. Almost before we had finished the work the radio started to crackle, "Hello, Dakota for one, how do you hear me, over". Our radio operator replied, "Hello, one for Dakota, I hear you loud and clear, over". Then, "Hello, Dakota for one, I have eleven chutes for you, over". We replied, "Hello, one for Dakota, drop your chutes over". The plane was visible at times as it swooped low over the DZ (Dropping Zone) area, but mostly we saw nothing until the chutes came down with a rush. They appeared to bounce over the ground for at least ten yards and then roll to a stop. The radio started up again, "Hello, one this is Dakota, I have dropped your chutes. Good morning". His Australian voice sounded very casual, almost as though he was delivering the morning papers or something. Why is it that when you get an air drop it is always the parachutes that are carrying the most important things that get stuck up in the tops of the trees? After checking the other chutes, we always seemed to be asking, where're the cans of beer, where're the biscuits, where're the chillies, etc. They were stuck up there and some we found impossible to get down. If we had chopped down the tree they were in, it would probably mean smashing the contents of the box into pieces. Yes, the socks were there, the spare trousers were there, the spare ammunition was there, but very often our "little extra something" supplies stayed stuck up a tree and very annoying it was, too.

This patch of jungle was very thick and when we decided to move back homewards the only way we found possible was to wade down a stream. Now the streams varied in depth and also were ideal places to be caught in ambush so you'd got to keep your eyes open. However the main problem was the depth of the stream, it would be about three feet deep most of the time, but then suddenly the man in front of you would disappear with a gurgle, and of course we all had a good laugh at him when he surfaced. Very funny, but not so funny when it was your turn to find a deep hole on the river bed a few minutes later. Ten or so miles walking down a river bed is not easy and we were glad when the jungle on the banks thinned out and we were able to return to dry land.

Before we started our deep jungle patrol, as I have said, we laid on two night ambushes.

There are leeches, snakes, centipedes and other things in the jungle, but they are not nearly as troublesome as the plague of mosquitoes and midges that swarm about you when you are ambushing on the jungle edge.

We set up our first ambush in the usual way, always ambush from one side of the track (if you are on both sides you are likely to fire at each other and that is very easily done), space your men out at about ten feet intervals. Keep your face and head and even hands, covered with a sarong. Only have your nose and eyes sticking out, that's the wise thing to do.

This first ambush was a lucky ambush, but we had to wait

from when we first got into position about five the previous evening until about six-thirty the following morning. There were three of them, we were about thirty yards in and the bandits, now believing that they were safe, had relaxed and were laughing and joking. All three were in full uniform, apart from hats and as they passed in front of my position, I could see their pale jungle faces quite clearly. We certainly obeyed the other golden rule that day which is, wait until the enemy are in the middle of the ambush before you open fire. Everybody did the right thing and in a matter of seconds it was all over. We had killed three bandits, the most we had ever got in one go, and soon we were relieving them of their shotguns, pistols and one hand grenade. They were also carrying rice, and other food in small quantities. It seemed as if they were on their way back to camp, but we didn't find it.

We sent two sections back with the bodies, one to carry and one to cover the carrying section, and then had to wait for them to get back. We had to wait more than thirty six hours, for they had to carry out to the main road, have a rest and then get back to us. The total distance that they covered was probably not more than seven miles, but they had to get a night's sleep in, didn't they? We laid an ambush two nights later on a different track but without any success. The only success was achieved by the mosquitoes and midges, who fed well. So we carried on patrolling, hoping to find the camp. The jungle is very quiet during the day and sometimes sounds and smells can be detected quite easily by a wary patrol. The terrorists were good at keeping quiet, but we were not. If you are to achieve anything like complete silence, you must use hand signals, don't talk and tread carefully. The jungle itself is very beautiful, with thousands of very tall trees, some white, others grey, in fact almost every colour you could think of. When they reached the roof of the jungle, hundreds of feet up, for they were searching for sunlight, they spread out in a sheaf of green which looked on from above as if one could almost walk on it. Many creepers, rattans and vines hang down from the trees and secondary jungle grows in between in some places. Not a lot of the bird life can be seen when walking through the jungle, for it is taking place above the roof or canopy at the very top and in bright sunlight. The light in deep jungle is very poor, you can see but not very well. One is always glad to strike thinner undergrowth because the sunlight can now strike through, warm everyone up a bit and make everything brighter and look more cheerful.

Mangrove swamps are to be avoided, they are dangerous from the sinking point of view, but worse than that are the very nasty big thorns that seem to be everywhere and can cause some very nasty wounds.

Whilst the jungle livens up at night when most of the animal life comes out to eat and play, it is also very dark. You literally can't see a hand in front of you and unless you keep directly behind the man in front, you are liable to fall into a very deep hole and do yourself an injury.

So the lesson is, don't travel around at night in deep jungle. Get some "kip" in, which means get your head down.

12. Was it the Police?

The Emergency in Malaya was not a war, it was worse than a war. Why do I say this? It is because the Geneva Convention says that in a war situation, either side should not kill any person who is either wounded or captured. It also says that either side must not deport any person from the other side who is taken prisoner or being held in custody.

We must understand that war had not been declared in Malaya and therefore the Geneva Convention rules did not apply.

Whilst we were told when we arrived there that the terrorists did not take prisoners (there is no record of them ever taking prisoners) once we had reconciled ourselves to that situation, it did not seem to be something that was in the forefront of our minds. Like in war, the average soldier seldom considers that he may be killed, wounded, or taken prisoner, it was just the same during the Emergency, we never consciously thought about it. It was always the others that got killed, wasn't it!

I may say this, but I'm sure that deep inside we knew that it was a do or die situation and that's how we played it. The terrorists were serious and so were we. We did deport many thousands of people during those times but, as the Geneva Convention did not apply, we were within our rights to do so.

The Emergency was officially declared on the 18th of July, 1948 and continued until July, 1960, but there is a case for saying that it continued after that and that there are still some sparks left.

During most of the Emergency, the Federation of Malaya Police was organised in the following way.

The police in each of the eleven states of Selangor, Penang,

Kedah, Perak, Malacca, Negri Sembilan, Kelantan, Trengganu, Pahang, Johor and Perlis were each supervised by a Chief Police Officer (CPO). Each police state was then divided into police circles supervised by an OSPC (Officer Supervising Police Circle) and then into small police districts, each one supervised by an OCPD (Officer Commanding Police District).

The strategy was that the regular police from Commissioner down to constable, who had remained in place since the pre-emergency days, plus recruits of inspectors and constables from the police depot, did the main police day to day work. CID (Criminal Investigations Department) was there to help them as they pursued and apprehended criminals in the normal way. The courts and prisons operated in the usual way and you could still get "booked" for speeding. Just because the police were involved in their day to day work did not mean that they were excluded from anti-terrorist operations or being the target for terrorist attack. The other side of the coin was the anti-terrorist work. Most of it was done by the police lieutenants and the Special Constables. Each police lieutenant (a rank just senior to a police inspector) came under the authority of an OCPD and a typical police district might contain ten or twelve police lieutenants. Each lieutenant supervised the work of about four to five hundred special constables in his division. Most of the SCs were guards on the tin mines, rubber estates or important buildings within the division. Some of the SCs also helped to man the police stations that may be contained in the division. These 24 hours per day guard duties took up most of the SCs' time. Any that could be "prised away" from the system were taken by the police lieutenants and trained up into jungle squads.

The jungle squads operated against any CTs within their areas and had considerable success. Statistics show that jungle squads led by P/Lts killed more terrorists than the British army. The army mostly operated in deep jungle whilst the police squads operated in rubber estates and on the jungle edge. They had the advantage of only moving on "information" about "sighted" bandits given to them by the local people. Later on, jungle forts were set up in deep jungle and again they were manned by police lieutenants and Special Constables.

Special Branch

Here we had a unit whose job it was to identify the enemy. They were led by superintendents, contract assistant superintendents, inspectors and sergeants. The contract ASPs were usually appointed for a three year period and could for example be experts in finger printing, photography, psychology etc., to give just a few examples. Their work, to put it simply, was detective work. They set out to compile and analyse the complete framework of the Communist Terrorist Organisation. They questioned everybody that they thought could give them useful information.

In each police district, bandits who surrendered or were captured were able to give a lot of useful information. Suspect terrorist sympathisers and other suspect helpers were also questioned. Infiltration into the CT organisation proved to be the best way of getting information, it was also the most dangerous. Some special branch officers even posed as captured terrorist sympathisers and were locked away with the real CTs in the detention camps, which was a very dangerous game.

An idea which was tried for a short time was the formation of jungle squads that were called Q squads. These security force squads disguised themselves as armed uniformed terrorists. Many of them of course had to be Chinese. The Q squad would enter a kampong and ask for food and then enquire about security force movements and finally they tried to obtain information from the kampong occupants about what the local terrorists were doing. The main dangers were accidentally meeting a security force patrol and because the Q squad movements had to be kept secret, they often had to "run for their lives". The other danger was that the locals might "see through" their disguises and inform the real local Communist terrorists of their suspicions.

It proved to be a good idea in theory but difficult to put into practice. Eventually it was regretfully abandoned.

As we have said, General Templer gave top priority to special branch work and very soon a complete picture of the terrorist organisation was obtained.

*　　*　　*　　*　　*　　*

Let us first look at how the combatants were deployed during the period. The Communist terrorists probably numbered between eight and ten thousand and were spread from north to south and from east to west. Their largest efforts were probably concentrated on Johor, Pahang, Perak and Selangor. Because of the size of the area which they tried to cover, they were probably very "thin on the ground", although some very large gangs were reported on occasions. Their weapons, as we have already said, were in a very poor state of repair and they were very poorly trained. This they made up for by being very brave and utterly ruthless.

The police, who took the brunt of the fighting all the way through, had a total strength of about sixty seven thousand when the fighting stopped. Of this, sixty seven thousand police, fifty thousand were Malays, one thousand one hundred and seventy seven were European (of which more than six hundred were police lieutenants), one thousand six hundred and twenty three Indians and Pakistanis, and one thousand four hundred and twenty five Chinese. They also had to try and cover the whole country. This was a twenty four hours a day job and because of this they were always fully stretched. The British army (British and Gurkha troops) had a total strength of about forty thousand deployed during that time. The Home Guard, who only had small numbers at the beginning, finally achieved a total strength of three hundred and fifty thousand. *(Please note that these figures were taken from the library of the High Commissioner, London)*

Terrorist incidents rose to their highest during the month of May, 1950, the incidents numbered five hundred and two for that month. We have examined most of the events which happened during those times.

There is no doubt in my mind that the police played the most important role in winning the Emergency. That is only my opinion and in this context, my heart goes out to the police special constables for, without them, we might have been on the losing side.

Another factor to consider is the rapid increase in Home Guard numbers during 1951 and 1952. General Templer "got it all together" and the rest was guts and determination by all concerned.

13. Army Experiences

It was the middle of 1953 and my three year contract with the police would soon be ending. The bandits were being quietened down and as I was only an "average" police lieutenant it seemed to me to be a long shot to expect them to offer me another three year contract.

General Templer was doing well and was respected by most people and even feared by some. There is no doubt that he had the confidence of the security forces. Templer had got very keen on integrating all sections of the community. He saw it as the only long-term strategy for the future. With this in mind, he decided to start up the Federation Forces and was delighted when a good number of Chinese were amongst the first recruits to enlist.

I wrote and asked if I could be considered for a commission in Templer's new army. Sir Hugh Stockwell was GOC (General Officer Commanding) Malayan Forces at the time and after seeing a few people and finally him, the commission was offered. I accepted gratefully, firstly because I would probably need a new contract and secondly, that if it was good enough for General Templer, then it was good enough for me. The local press made a big fuss about Templer's first officers in the Federation Forces and soon more recruits were coming in. The post that I was to fill was Signals Officer of the 1st Battalion of the Federation Regiment (an Infantry unit).

A Signals Officer in a unit like this is responsible for making sure that everyone in the unit can talk to anyone else in that unit. Every platoon (about thirty to forty men) had a radio and the main control radio was at battalion headquarters. Wherever the platoons went, the control set had to be able to contact them on their radios. We have a model 19 set at

Control and they have model 38 sets. Whenever possible I also organised telephone communications between them. In the regiment we used speech RT (Radio Telephone) – we spoke to them and they spoke to us. We could use WT (Wireless Telegraph) if we wanted, that's morse code, and we sometimes did when communications were generally difficult but usually it was RT. In the police we always used morse code when we sent messages because they usually had to be sent over long distances and weak signals could be more easily "picked out" on WT. The only time the police used "voice" was when they were using VHF (Very High Frequency) sets in the town for the 99 calls with the police mobile patrols.

I am proud to say that I used a little trick to keep in touch with the platoons. Contact in deep jungle was always difficult and so the plan was, always take with you about twenty yards of covered telephone cable, find a nearby stream or river and erect the aerial (the telephone cable) about ten feet above the surface. The secret was that the river acted as a reflector for the incoming and outgoing radio waves and also the space above rivers usually contained less trees and foliage than in other places that you might pick. Wood and trees do block radio waves and so the clearer the passage for the signals, the better. That was the job that I was going to do with the army. I was to have the Signals platoon and they turned out to be the best. They would do anything, go anywhere, and were completely reliable, all thirty of them. I knew that I would be able to do the job and looked forward to the challenge. I would be doing the same kind of work, but wearing a different uniform, a kind of transfer from police work to army work. I then went back to England for a short leave. Because I had accepted the job here in Malaya I had to find the return fare out of my own pocket.

The return journey from Malaya to England on a British Airways aeroplane was a strange experience. To say that I just felt light-headed would be an understatement of my mental condition as I sat on that plane. I knew where I was, but it did not seem to match the reality of the situation. The air hostesses were not walking in between the seats and down the passageways, they seemed to be rolling along, almost gliding and there were other persons on the plane but I seemed almost unaware of their presence. My jumbled thoughts seemed incapable of adjusting themselves. As I flew another thought occurred to me, was I mad? It only stayed for a few brief seconds, but it was there. These morbid thoughts passed and gradually I pulled myself together. As we touched down in London the other passengers began to look real and I felt a lot better. Being prepared for any eventuality had probably left its mark. Going to sleep at night (every night) with your hand around the butt of a half-cocked 9mm automatic pistol was very habit forming. Why half-cocked? Well, ask any army man the difference between the relatively quiet sound when fully cocking a pistol that is half cocked already and the loud click made by fully cocking a pistol. The extra noise made would certainly give my position away and take that fraction of a second longer. It may even cost me my life. Sounds far-fetched, doesn't it? Well, it isn't, it's true. Maybe we were being ultra-cautious. I'm certainly not ashamed to admit that all the time I was very cautious. Dead men tell no tales. You will laugh again when I tell you that years later a car journey through a peaceful Welsh valley which had cuttings on either side like some roads where we were being ambushed always made my heart race faster.

Well I suppose we'd better get back to where the real action is. The journey was on the P&O Liner *Corfu* and it was to cost me ninety pounds (It may not sound like a lot of money to you, but it did to me). Oh, incidentally, if you want to have the holiday of a life-time take a P&O cruise, it must be P&O. Good food, good service, good everything. Go on a big one (at least 18,000 tons), and sit back and enjoy it. Twenty one days, that's what it was going to take us to get to Penang from Southampton, and it was twenty one days of heaven. We spent the time doing what all young men the world over do, we chased the girls whenever we could. We even devised a system whereby the older (girls) would iron our shirts in exchange for a smile and a chat. Eventually, we went too far. We got roped in on the entertainment committee looking after entertainment for the children onboard. "What games can we have the children playing?" asked one of the parents, they were mostly mothers. "How about Hop Scotch near the edge of the ship's deck?" said one of the lads from my cabin. This was greeted by grunts and groans from the mothers. I then put my foot right in it by jokingly suggesting "Walking the Plank". That did it, they almost threw us off the committee!

The 1st Battalion, the Federation Regiment, were stationed at Taiping in Perak. We had just started the training of about five hundred recruits which included a goodly number of Chinese youths. Was Templer's dream coming true? We could always rely on support from the Indians and the Malays. Taiping is a very happy town and situated about an hour's drive from Penang. It has a jail where some of the town's British army personnel (they were camped just outside the town) would give up some of their free time and come and play badminton with the more trusted prisoners and some of the surrendered bandits that were there. There is a swimming pool very near to the jungle edge on the east side, which has a very long, high slide into it. You have to be brave to go on that slide and I didn't. The local cinema was very good.

The main Padang was where all the sports were played, football, rugby and cricket. We eventually held our passing-out parade on that Padang. The best thing that I saw on that Padang was a parade of the local Red Cross, which included quite a lot of pretty girls, a very nice sight for a lonely soldier. Our officers' mess was a two-storey house, just off the Padang and we had about three senior officers there, three national service officers (all ex-public school) and little me, the working-class lad playing at soldiers. Nothing worth writing home about ever happened here. It was just dirty looks from the senior officers whilst we dutifully tolerated their inane conversations over the evening meal and so to bed. It was the cinema once a week and a swim in the pool on Sunday afternoon that cemented every uneventful week which passed as mess life. There are plenty of gibbons in the secondary jungle just to the east of the town and their early morning calls usually signalled the start of another day. The calls that they make are something like the sound made by an English Owl, but of course very much louder, ooh, ooh, they would cry, and the answers came back like echoes.

Turn to the right when you come out of our mess and you're on our main parade ground, and the recruits' billets are just a bit further down on the right. The training that the recruits had to go through would have defied any rules laid down by the Geneva Convention. Tough? I'd say it was very, very tough. They were kept drilling, running and kit cleaning from five thirty every morning (except Sunday) until about eight every night. There was a regular "kit layout" inspection every morning at eight and to avoid any punishment that they may receive for untidy kit layout they did the following. Their kits were laid out perfectly on their beds but they didn't use the beds for sleeping in (they might disturb the kit layout), instead they all slept on the floor every night, yes, all 500 of them. I'm sure that quite a few tears were shed by those tough boys as they tried to settle their tired, aching bodies onto a hard barrack-room floor. There was just one senior officer there who was not short of a few original ideas, a regular soldier who was liked by most of us, but his genius was not recognised by his seniors and he was overlooked for the promotion which he probably deserved.

There were reports (unofficial) that there had been some

fighting amongst the recruits when they went into Taiping on their nights out. One of our sergeants came to us a few days later and told us the full story. There was fighting going on in town amongst the recruits at night and by all reports it was the same three or four who always started (and finished) the trouble, if you follow my meaning. When our genius found out, he was livid and assembled all the battalion and told them to fall in in "horseshoe fashion". Then into the centre of the horseshoe came the battalion boxing team, and the three lads who were at the centre of the trouble. On the command, "start training", the team split into three or four parts and each did a different kind of training, first exercises, then shadow boxing, then sparring, and finally a three minute round in the ring with the battalion's boxing champion. This went on for about half an hour and we all watched with our mouths open. Change over, change over, shouted the staff sergeant PTI (Physical Training Instructor) as they went through their routines. Eventually, it came the turn of the unfortunate specially selected recruits to do their three minutes with the champion. They learnt their lesson that morning and we didn't have any more fights in town after that, well, not too many.

We were moving to Butterworth which is just opposite the island of Penang. The camp was not too far from the ferry point in Butterworth. Just go through Butterworth town and take the coast road north, the camp is only about half a mile distance, on the left hand side. We were in between the main road and the sea.

The camp had been previously used by the Manchester Regiment (a British army unit) and it was perfectly sited. The sea was twenty to thirty yards away on one side and the road to Penang Island on the other. We had plenty of room in the officers' and sergeants' messes, good quarters for up to five hundred men and also excellent dining rooms and cook houses.

We had to organise separate cooking facilities for some of

the food, for the Muslim Malays are not allowed to eat pork and they have to watch other things that their religion does not permit. Apart from this, cooking was easy, everyone ate rice and vegetables. I didn't get on very well with a new senior officer who came into the company. He was very senior and his wishes had to be complied with. He ordered that only English was to be spoken by officers when talking to the troops. My Malay was good enough for everyday conversation but I was caught out one day. I had the company on parade, and after inspecting them and their weapons, I decided that they weren't good enough, especially their dirty rifles and other weapons. I proceeded to tell them off in Malay. They were strangely quiet and I thought that my telling them off had worked. I turned around and there was the reason for their quietness; that certain senior officer was there and had heard every word of my Malay. He could not speak any Malay and had failed his Malay language course, so the rumour went. Anyway, his deep frown told the story and I put myself down for a "black mark".

Now that we had become operational we started patrolling. The first work was in the Bukit Mertajam area. One of 'A' Company's sets went faulty and their spare had low batteries and so my "friend" told me to take two signallers out to the company and get them back into action. We were still in contact with 'A' Company, but the signals were weak and he probably had a case. Take two men, did he say, yes that was it. I sensed a dodgy situation may develop. The two signallers, the spare set and myself were dropped off on the main road and then we had to make a three mile journey along the jungle edge to a pre-arranged rendezvous. Now I knew that bandit foraging parties usually moved in twos and threes and that any of our people (like Home Guards and police jungle squads) who saw two or three figures lurking on the jungle edge, would shoot first and ask questions later. Anyhow, all went well and I was worrying for nothing.

Suddenly, there was a rustling from the jungle edge and the 'A' Company rendezvous party emerged with big grins on their faces.

A mile later I was in the 'A' Company base camp. The Malay signaller soon fixed up the set and we joined the rest for a bath in the stream and a glorious curry for supper. Now who wants a holiday when you can have luxury like this? It was a very comfortable camp, the outstanding personality being the Malay Sergeant Major. Now I was used to seeing him on parade back at Butterworth but somehow or other, I did not expect to see him in the jungle. He was there, and his six feet tall frame seemed to be everywhere. He was a very cheerful man and looked every inch a soldier. I saw him supervising the cooking of the rice for our curry and he was even on the "set" at one stage. The outstanding feature about him was his infectious smile, but behind that smile lay a very tough man.

One of my friends there (a Second Lieutenant Patrol Leader) who later made Brigadier General, was pleased to see me and I was pleased to see him. That first night we slept on the edge of the camp on the jungle floor and talked and talked until we both fell into a deep sleep. I hung around for two days and then went back to that place called civilization.

It had got "a bit much" in the officers' mess, dinner nights on three or four nights a week, all dressed up, of course, and these limited our Penang visits to maybe once a week. I couldn't quite see the point in it all and thought we should concentrate all our efforts on killing bandits. By this time, a lot of new officers were arriving fresh from England where they had been doing training courses. They were given jobs to do in the Company. Now most Malays are quiet and un-assuming, but one of the new officers was extremely quiet and very unassuming. He was smaller than the average Malay and very slim. The most striking feature about him was his good looks and his shy, retiring manner. When we talked in the mess, his eyes used to flick up and down, showing that he really was interested in what you were saying. I mention this officer because he went on to become a full General. Forces people who read this will know who I mean.

We in the Signals platoon were very proud of our "Yargi" aerial. To the technically-minded people it was horizontally polarised, three quarter landa aerial, with a twin feeder connecting it to the transceiver. In other words, if you "shin up" several coconut trees to about fifty feet off the ground and put up four pieces of telephone wire in the shape of four "L"s and then position them together so that they look like an "H" when looked at from the ground, that's it. Make sure that the bare wire doesn't touch the trees and connect it to the set with a double length of cable. This aerial gave us good distance and we could get almost anywhere with it.

One of the sergeants, a friendly sort, asked me if I would act as Defending Officer for a recruit who had just returned from his kampong after being AWOL (absent without leave) for about three months. When I accepted, the Adjutant was told and I began to make my preparations. It was a district court martial and it was to be held at our camp in Butterworth. The Adjutant (a British army captain) was to be the Prosecuting Officer and I, now a Lieutenant, was to be the Defending Officer. I went to see the lad in the guard room and had several talks with him. It appeared that he had gone back to his kampong on seven days' leave and fallen in love with an older woman. When he eventually returned, he was dressed in his uniform. Because he had come back voluntarily and in uniform, he could not be charged with desertion. One of the things that he told me was that the woman "had put a charm on him" and that he found that he was unable to leave the village. True or not, it sounded like a good story and after reviewing who the Officers of the Court were to be, it sounded hopeful. There were three Majors on the Bench, two had only been in the country for a couple of months, and the other was a regular army major who had come to us from the Malay Regiment. I kept quiet about my defence tactics but briefed the sergeant well.

The boy (well, he was about eighteen years old) was put before the court. The Adjutant attacked him without mercy. He was a disgrace to the Regiment and deserved the maximum punishment that the court could give (one hundred and twelve days in military prison). The soldier looked visibly shaken and was very upset as he told his story to the court. Everyone seemed to be listening, but the silence that reigned said that not many believed him. The Adjutant now had a flicker of a smile on his face.

The sergeant's name was called and he was a very smart soldier, in fact he was a drill sergeant. His entrance into the court impressed everyone, even the Officers of the Court sat upright in their seats. "Sergeant", I said, "what kind of recruit soldier is the Accused?" "A very good soldier, Sir," he answered, "probably one of the best in my squad". The Court Officers blinked and sat up even straighter. Even the Adjutant, who thought he'd got the whole thing sewn up, began to pay attention. "Would you think that this soldier would go willingly absent without leave?" I asked. "No, Sir" he answered. He saluted the court with one of the smartest salutes I have ever seen and on the command of the Sergeant Major, marched out. It was my turn now. Turning to them I said, "Here we have a young soldier who went on seven days' leave and didn't come back until he reported into the guard room long after he was due back". "I'll tell you the truth about what happened to him" I said. "When he arrived in his kampong, a woman, older than him, somehow gave him a love potion. This may seem incredible to you, but this love potion was given to him and he found himself unable to leave and unable to get out of the situation. This does not seem possible to us," I said, looking straight into the faces of the Court Officers, "but out here these love potions are given quite often". They blinked, especially the two that had only just come out to

Malaya, and all three mouths opened a little. "You have heard the sergeant describe the recruit as an excellent recruit who should make a good soldier" I said. "He came back and reported into the guard room smartly dressed and ready to resume his duties as if he'd done no wrong. These were not the actions of a guilty man, but one who was very confused. I put it to you that these were exceptional circumstances and ask you to deal leniently with this good recruit".

Sixty eight days field punishment (full pack drill for most of the daylight hours) to be done at Butterworth was their verdict. The Adjutant was not pleased, but we were. I saw the sergeant in the camp later that day and as we passed he gave me a smile and a knowing wink.

Life was not too dull in the army but you didn't have the freedom of action that life in the police gave you. There was a mess routine, which was a pain in the neck, not so much the dinner nights and dressing up for dinner but the rituals which had to be gone through before and after. I suppose it was the "pecking order" in the mess that was so irksome, the CO, the Mess President, the Adjutant, the multitude of majors, etc., and we juniors just sitting there like parrots on perches awaiting permission to move or even to speak. It was different from the police lieutenants' mess where everyone was the same rank and we were all glad to be alive whenever we met.

Two incidents made it clearer to me one night. We had about half an hour or so before we were due to go into dinner when an unshaved face of a popular major appeared, sticking his head around the door. He had been on patrol for about ten days and looked a bit the worse for wear. He was advised to go to his room and some sandwiches would be sent to him, they said. He wouldn't quite fit in with us stuffed dummies, maybe that was why they didn't say "come in" and give him a drink. He'd only been out in the jungle leading a company against the enemy, but protocol had its way and off to bed he went. Maybe that was the army way, but it didn't seem quite right to me.

We had guests in the mess, never more than two or three, but we were supposed to never leave the mess at nights when guests were present without the permission of the senior officer present. It was usually the local OCPD (Officer Commanding Police District) or an officer from RAF Butterworth who came and this same night we had one guest who at midnight was talking to a group of senior officers over in one corner. The rest of us were dutifully trying to stay awake, our hands holding a drink that was now warm, for we had been clasping it for about an hour. One o'clock came and we decided that we had done our duty and because we all had work to do the following day, we started slipping off to bed, one by one (without permission). About half an hour later every door was knocked on and I think that most of them got dressed and went back into the mess. I didn't go and so I probably lost another bonus point.

More national service junior officers arrived (two of them) and we were determined to have a lark with them. I normally went out to Penang, when able, with the Medical Officer, a down-to-earth Welshman, with a wry sense of humour. We planned a night out with the new pair. They said that they wanted to go for some Chinese food. Did we know anything about Chinese food? Did we? We knew everything. In fact, we spoke good Chinese and had been to most of the best Chinese restaurants that there were. Lies, of course, all lies, but they looked impressed. Across the ferry in my Ford Consul, what a good car, and we duly arrived in the centre of Georgetown, the capital of Penang.

One of them spotted a restaurant at the side of the street. Did we know this restaurant? Did we know it? We knew them all, we said, and this particular one we'd visited several times and it was very good (still telling lies). Looking at the menu we saw that it was completely printed in Chinese. Trying to look calm we asked them what they would like to eat. "We'll have what you usually have" they said. The Medical Officer's eyes nearly popped out of their sockets. Luckily, there were some numbers written in English style alongside the dishes. "We usually have number 57 here," said I, picking one from near the middle of the menu. "Let's have four number fifty sevens then" said one of the new boys. The meal was quite good and the newcomers were impressed. I "borrowed" one of the menus and the next day asked one of our Chinese officers what we had ordered. "It's the intestines of chicken mixed with python meat" he said. I still don't know who had the last laugh, do you?

I had a short leave in KL and called into the control room to say hello. I wasn't being nosey, but lying in full view on the desk was a signal which read as follows (apparently the police had not yet realised I had left the force), "The following police lieutenants are offered further contracts". My name, because it began with "A" was at the top of the list. You may remember Pesagi, we mentioned him earlier when he had a run-in with Templer. Well, things weren't going too well for him. I spotted him on Batu Road one evening and he didn't look too good. He told me that he had left the police, something about a driving offence. Anyhow, I took him to the KK Hotel and got him fixed up because I don't think he was very well fixed for money. Well it seemed that way, maybe I was wrong. I then shot off to see an ex-police lieutenant friend of mine called Arthur who was managing a rubber estate about fifty miles north of Kuala Lumpur. Arthur knew Pesagi as well as I did and he also knew a Chinese owner of Sungei Triang Estate who was desperate for a European presence on the estate. It was alive with bandits, and so armed with a reference from Arthur as to Pesagi's character, etc. I went to meet the Chinese owner in Seremban. It's true to say that he knew the area very well, he was offered the job and took it. I don't know how he's getting on, he might still be there.

As a point of interest, the British army used Dyaks, a fierce people from Borneo, as trackers. The Dyaks had a distinctive way of looking and operating. Very often, it was reported, that when they had ambushed successfully they would ask the soldiers if they could go in with their *parangs* (large knives) and behead some of the enemy. They have a distinctive tattoo on their necks. It is drawn on the front of their necks and has a neck, body, two arms and two legs, the idea being that if they themselves get beheaded then their head will still have a body.

Whilst we were setting up camp in Pokok Sena about thirty miles from the Siamese border in Kedah we had time on our hands and were looking around under some fruit trees. We saw hundreds of flying foxes hanging upside down from the branches of the trees. One of the lads got one down and it screeched and screeched. It had a head that looked like a fox's but smaller, of course, a very small body, with enormous leathery bat shaped wings. It lived on the fruit that it got from the fruit trees where it slept for most of the day. The wingspan was about two metres. After we had looked at it we took it back to the trees and put it back in bed. We saw some of the local Tamils catching them one night. At night they fly around and around the fruit trees and then settle down for a bite to eat and then fly around and around again. The Tamils were hoisting a large net directly in their flight path, catching one or two at a time, quickly lowering the net, getting hold of them and with a quick slit of the throat they were then put into a bag. They told us that they got about one dollar fifty for each one so obviously someone found them good eating. Could they have been number fifty seven at Penang?

A company had contacted three terrorists and killed one, the op/immediate signal said. Then it was hurriedly delivered to the top. Within half an hour my Malay Signaller was given a signal to send to all platoons of the company. It congratulated them and gave them the location of the success. Follow up the other two and get them, was the message. The Signaller was quite upset when I asked him to wait a bit. He had been trained to get op/immediate messages off straight away and any delay could not be tolerated. Anyhow, I took the message with me and asked if it had to be sent, pointing out that an eight figure map reference had been given and that a full company of troops converging onto such a small spot on the map in deep jungle was not such a good idea. I left it with one of the senior officers and then more or less disappeared. I never did check if that message was actually sent. I suppose I shouldn't have queried it, but I did. I don't suppose it earned me any bonus points, whichever way it went.

It was the 1st Battalion's first kill and we were all very pleased. I had now done about eighteen months but had decided that there was too much bickering on high to suit my taste. It was not what I had come out to Malaya for; it was no longer the fear of the unseen bandit but the unknown sneak dropping you in the soup. Give me the bandits anyday, I thought. You can judge from this that I had decided to resign my commission.

Just before that day we had about twenty recruit signallers attached to us for training. They were helping us to check stores and the old platoon were doing most of the work because they knew what they were doing. The cigarette ration arrived, fifty cigarettes each, in a tin. I said to them all, "Leave them there, we'll be finished in about ten minutes, get them then". It made sense to my lads but not to the new recruits, for almost immediately, when my back was turned, they packed up work, opened their cigarettes and began sending up clouds of smoke. My lads were furious and I was not very pleased. My platoon said, "You'll have to teach them a lesson, Sir" and I agreed. "Fall them in Corporal" I said. "Yes, Sir" he said and rushed over and ordered them to fall in. They marched off just outside the signal office and went across the open ground under our Yargi aerial. They looked as though they were marching in an awkward way and so I shouted to the Corporal, "Double them up, Corporal". "Double march" he ordered. Now the lad in the middle rank at the front didn't want to double march and carried on just marching. The result was, as you can imagine, just chaos. They finished up in an untidy mess and were eventually stopped by the now furious Corporal. I shouted again, "Fall in two men" and then shouted to the Corporal to double him off to the Guard Room. As they say, his feet didn't touch the ground, they literally lifted him up by his elbows and ran him to the Guard Room. I let him out a few hours later and hoped he'd learned his lesson. You're not supposed to put a man in the Guard Room unless you intend to bring charges against him, but I was leaving within days, so it didn't matter much.

It was my going away "tea party" the next afternoon – you know, tea, sticky buns, and speeches, mostly tea and speeches. First the Staff Sergeant, then the Sergeant and then the Corporals, and then a few more, all of them gave a little speech about me, very nice and much appreciated. Then a young Chinese Signaller stood up at the back and said he wanted to speak. He was howled down because he was young and relatively new to the platoon, but he was determined to say his piece. His speech went something like this, "When I am coming to Signalling Platoon I am going into Signalling Office and there I am meeting Signalling Officer, Mr Andrew. He is standing up and shaking me by the hand and saying I am very pleased to meet you. This making my heart very happy and so I am so sorry he is leaving. Thank you". I don't know if the tears rolled down my cheeks but they were in my eyes and I still get a lump in my throat when I think about my platoon. Could there be a better reward than the loyalty they had all shown?

They paid my fare home, thank you and so my association with Malaya had finished.

> Good luck Malaysia
> Selamat Jalan
> Jaga Baik-Baik.

The author poses for the camera outside the Signals office.

Inspecting the guard.

The author, inside the Signals office.

The Red Cross parade on the main padang at Taiping.

The Signals platoon. The author is seated on the front row, eighth from the left.

Glossary

Ada cukup brani?	Are you brave enough?
Ada cukup kuat?	Are you strong enough?
Ada takut?	Are you afraid?
bandits	a word used by the Security Forces when talking about the Communist Terrorists
bashas	jungle sleeping shelter
bed fellows	sleeping companions
BB	Bukit Bintang (Star Hill)
Bench	the adjudicating judges
boarder	a student who eats and lives at his college
bit much	rather excessive
black mark	an indication of disapproval, failure
berhenti	halt (stop)
Bukit Hitam	Black Hill
CID	Criminal Investigations Department
cold feet	fear
CPO	Chief Police Officer
CT	Communist Terrorist
double march	run
Dato Ampat	village leader
diehard	a person of fixed and stubborn beliefs
daredevil	a person who is not afraid to take risks
drug scene	an area where people smoke and take drugs
easy meat	easy to overcome
flipped his lid	gone crazy
flogged	beaten with a leather whip
feet didn't touch	when he is being arrested

field day	free expression occasion
gazetted	recorded on the government's gazetted officers list
get your head down	go to sleep
gibbon	an animal belonging to the ape family
GOC	General Officer Commanding
horseshoe fashion	assembled in the shape of a horseshoe
HMS	Her Majesty's Ship
hung on	stayed
ICI	Imperial Chemical Industries
i/c	in charge of
jaga baik baik	take care
jalan perlahan perlahan	travel slowly
kampongs	malay villages
kedai	shop(s)
King's House	the residence of the High Commissioner
kip	sleep
KL	Kuala Lumpur, the capital of Malaysia
magazine	ammunition container attached to weapon
mahu masuk. . .?	do you want to join ...?
makings	everything that is necessary for developing (into)
mate	friend
MCP	Malayan Communist Party
Min Yuen	Chinese people who helped the Communists
MPAJA	Malayan People's Anti-Japanese Army
MT	Motor Transport
national service	compulsory military experience for young men
orang utan	large gorilla type monkey
OC	Officer Commanding

OCPD	Officer Commanding Police District
OC Train	Officer Commanding Train
Ops	Operations
Ops Room	Operations Room
OSPC	Officer Supervising Police Circle
picnic	an enjoyable outdoor experience
PC	Police Constable
P/Lt.	Police Lieutenant
PT	phyical training
pot shot	a quickly aimed shot
P&O	Peninsular and Oriental
RAF	Royal Air Force
REME	Royal Electrical and Mechanical Engineers
Sakai	the original inhabitants of Malaya
Selamat Jalan	Have a good journey
salt of the earth	a reliable, sensible person
Saya belum kawin lagi	I am not married yet
SC	Special Constable
SEP	Surrendered Enemy Personnel
seedier	rough and unruly
Sikh	a religious sect from India and Pakistan whose members wear turbans on their heads
Sten gun	a small machine gun
stint	period of duty
stuck	given a job you don't want
yoke	restrictive control
Zionists	a group of terrorists who fought against the British to obtain control of Palestine